Elixir Programming

From Basics to Expert Proficiency

Contents

Introduction

Elixir is a dynamic, functional language designed for building scalable and maintainable applications. Created by José Valim, it leverages the robust and fault-tolerant capabilities of the Erlang VM while providing a more approachable syntax and a rich toolset for modern software development.

The purpose of this book is to equip you with the knowledge required to design, develop, and deploy Elixir applications proficiently. Starting from basic concepts and gradually moving towards advanced topics, the content is organized to help you build a solid understanding of the language and its ecosystem.

Elixir has grown significantly in popularity due to its powerful concurrency model, inbuilt fault tolerance, and ability to handle distributed systems effortlessly. It is particularly well-suited for web development, real-time services, and applications where performance and reliability are critical.

In the initial chapters, you will become acquainted with the basics of Elixir, covering its syntax, data structures, and fundamental programming constructs. These early sections are crucial as they lay the foundation for better comprehension of more advanced topics discussed later in the book.

As you advance, you will delve into the functional aspects of Elixir, exploring how to write and structure functions and modules. One of the core strengths of Elixir is its seamless concurrency model, which we will cover in detail, including processes, message-passing, and leveraging the Actor model. This will be followed by a comprehensive examination of the Open Telecom Platform (OTP) framework, which provides a set of design principles and tools for building concurrent and distributed applications in Elixir.

Project management is another critical area addressed in this book, focusing on Mix, the build tool that facilitates testing, compiling, and managing dependencies in Elixir projects. Testing is covered extensively, emphasizing the importance of robust and reliable software.

The book also explores metaprogramming, giving you insights into how to write macros and modify code at compile time. This level of abstraction is powerful but requires a clear understanding to avoid common pitfalls.

Finally, the book will guide you through deploying and maintaining Elixir applications in a production environment. From performance optimization and monitoring to ensuring security and scalability, these sections are vital for delivering professional-grade applications.

By the end of this book, you should possess a thorough understanding of Elixir and its ecosystem, empowering you to create efficient, fault-tolerant, and scalable applications. The knowledge acquired will not only make you proficient in Elixir but also provide you with a greater appreciation of the principles of concurrent and functional programming.

Chapter 1

Introduction to Elixir

This chapter provides an overview of Elixir, highlighting its origins and advantages. It covers the initial setup for developing in Elixir and introduces the interactive shell (IEx) for executing Elixir commands. Readers will become familiar with Elixir's basic syntax, conventions, and fundamental constructs, including variables and basic data types. The chapter also emphasizes essential elements like comments, documentation, and tools within the Elixir ecosystem, culminating in a first practical example of coding in Elixir.

1.1 Why Elixir? A Brief History

Elixir is a functional, concurrent, general-purpose programming language that runs on the Erlang Virtual Machine (BEAM). Developed by José Valim, a former member of the Ruby on Rails core team, Elixir was first released in 2011. Valim aimed to create a language that could handle large-scale and low-latency distributed systems while providing elegant syntax and powerful tooling.

Elixir's roots are deeply embedded in the Erlang ecosystem, a language and runtime developed by Ericsson in the 1980s. Erlang was designed to support distributed, fault-tolerant, soft real-time systems with high availability requirements. These characteristics make Erlang an ideal foundation for telecommunication systems, database servers, and instant messaging applications. However, Erlang's syntax and conventions can be unconventional and intimidating for developers coming from other programming backgrounds.

Recognizing Erlang's robustness and the need for a more approachable syntax, Valim designed Elixir to leverage the Erlang VM's capabilities while introducing a modern, extensible, and developer-friendly language. Elixir features a syntax inspired by Ruby, facilitating easier adoption for developers familiar with object-oriented and imperative programming paradigms.

Elixir's design goals include:

- **Scalability**: By inheriting the lightweight process model of Erlang, Elixir supports massive concurrency. Elixir processes are isolated, lightweight, and managed by the BEAM, allowing millions of processes to run concurrently without significant overhead.
- **Fault-tolerance**: Elixir adopts Erlang's "let it crash" philosophy, wherein processes are designed to fail and restart gracefully. This approach simplifies error management and enhances system resilience.
- **Maintainability**: Elixir's syntax and tooling aim to improve developer productivity and code readability. Macros and metaprogramming capabilities allow developers to extend the language and build domain-specific languages (DSLs).
- **Productivity**: The Elixir ecosystem includes powerful tools such as Mix (a build tool) and Hex (a package manager), which streamline project management and dependency resolution.
- **Interoperability**: Elixir seamlessly integrates with Erlang libraries and can invoke functions written in Erlang, providing access to a mature and extensive ecosystem.

Elixir's functional programming paradigm emphasizes immutability and first-class functions. This differs from the object-oriented paradigm, which focuses on encapsulating state and behavior within objects. In Elixir, data is immutable, and functions are first-class citizens, promoting a declarative coding style. These principles contribute to the language's simplicity and predictability, making code easier to reason about and test.

To illustrate Elixir's functional nature, consider the following example where we define a function to calculate the factorial of a number. In

Elixir, recursion is a common pattern for such computations due to the absence of traditional looping constructs like for and while:

```
defmodule Math do
  def factorial(0), do: 1
  def factorial(n) when n > 0 do
    n * factorial(n - 1)
  end
end

Math.factorial(5)
```

In this code, the factorial/1 function demonstrates pattern matching and recursion, both core concepts in Elixir.

Elixir also simplifies the development of concurrent applications. Leveraging the BEAM's concurrency model, Elixir allows developers to spawn and manage processes effortlessly. Here we demonstrate spawning a process and sending a message:

```
spawn(fn ->
  receive do
    msg ->
      IO.puts("Message received: \#\{msg\}")
  end
end)

send(self(), :hello)
```

In this example, the spawn/1 function creates a new process that waits to receive a message. When the message :hello is sent to the process, it is printed to the console.

Elixir's macro system provides metaprogramming capabilities, enabling developers to write code that generates code. This feature allows for powerful abstractions and DSLs. Here is a simple macro example that generates a function to greet a user:

```
defmodule Greetings do
  defmacro hello(name) do
    quote do
      def unquote(:"hello_\#\{name\}")() do
        IO.puts("Hello, \#\{unquote(name)\}!")
      end
    end
  end
end

defmodule Greeter do
  require Greetings
  Greetings.hello(:john)
end

Greeter.hello_john()
```

This code dynamically generates the hello_john/0 function, which prints a personalized greeting.

Elixir's creation was driven by a need to balance concurrency, maintainability, and productivity in modern software development. By combining the strengths of Erlang and introducing a more expressive syntax, Elixir has become a solution for building scalable, maintainable, and resilient systems.

1.2 Setting Up Elixir

Setting up Elixir on your development machine involves a series of steps to ensure that you have all the necessary tools and dependencies installed for an optimal environment. The following instructions cover the setup for the most widely used operating systems: Linux, macOS, and Windows.

Linux

For most Linux distributions, Elixir can be installed using the package manager. However, to ensure you have the latest version, it is often better to use the official repository. Here is a guided step-by-step process:

- First, ensure that you have Erlang/OTP installed, as Elixir runs on the Erlang VM.
- Add the Erlang Solutions repository to get the latest versions of Erlang and Elixir:

```
wget https://packages.erlang-solutions.com/erlang-solutions_2.0_all.deb
sudo dpkg -i erlang-solutions_2.0_all.deb
sudo apt-get update
```

- Install the latest version of Erlang/OTP:

```
sudo apt-get install -y esl-erlang
```

- Finally, install Elixir:

```
sudo apt-get install -y elixir
```

macOS

For macOS users, Homebrew is the easiest and most straightforward way to install Elixir.

- Ensure you have Homebrew installed. If not, you can install it using the following command:

```
/bin/bash -c "$(curl -fsSL https://raw.githubusercontent.com/Homebrew/install/
    HEAD/install.sh)"
```

- Once Homebrew is installed, you can install Elixir by executing:

```
brew install elixir
```

Windows

Setting up Elixir on Windows can be done using the precompiled installer provided by the Elixir team.

- Download the installer from the official Elixir website: https://elixir-lang.org/install.html.
- Run the installer and follow the instructions.

Verifying the Installation

After installing Elixir, you should verify that the installation was successful by checking the installed versions of Erlang and Elixir. Open your terminal (or Command Prompt on Windows), and execute the following commands:

```
erl -version
elixir -v
```

The expected output should resemble the following (version numbers may vary):

```
Erlang/OTP 24 [erts-12.0] [source] [64-bit] [smp:4:4] [ds:4:4:10] [async-threads:1] [hipe]
Elixir 1.12.2 (compiled with Erlang/OTP 24)
```

This output confirms that Erlang and Elixir are correctly installed on your system.

Setting Up an Editor

While you can use any text editor to write Elixir code, several editors offer enhanced support for Elixir through plugins or built-in functionalities. Below are recommendations for various popular editors:

- Visual Studio Code: Install the ElixirLS plugin, which provides IDE features such as debugging, IntelliSense, and more.
- Atom: Linters and syntax highlighting can be added via packages like language-elixir and ide-elixir.
- Emacs: Utilize the elixir-mode and alchemist packages for a highly integrated development environment.
- Vim: The elixir-vim plugin provides syntax highlighting and other editing features. Coupling it with ale can also introduce linting capabilities.

To configure the above extensions and plugins, follow the respective installation instructions provided in each editor's documentation or plugin repository.

With the environment set up correctly, you will now be able to utilize the Elixir Interactive Shell (IEx) and start writing and executing code efficiently.

1.3 The Elixir Interactive Shell (IEx)

The Elixir Interactive Shell, known as IEx, is a powerful tool for Elixir developers. It allows real-time code execution, providing a convenient environment for testing, debugging, and exploring language features. IEx is akin to the REPL (Read-Eval-Print Loop) found in other programming languages, facilitating an interactive programming experience.

To start IEx, open your terminal and type:

```
$ iex
```

Upon execution, the IEx shell will start, showing a prompt similar to the following:

```
Interactive Elixir (1.11.4) - press Ctrl+C to exit (type h() ENTER for help)
iex(1)>
```

The iex(1)> prompt indicates that the shell is ready to accept commands. The number inside the parentheses increases with each command executed, reflecting the history of commands.

Basic Usage

IEx supports the execution of Elixir expressions and can be used to inspect their outputs immediately. For example:

```
iex(1)> 1 + 2
3
```

In this example, IEx evaluates the expression 1 + 2 and returns the result 3.

Accessing Documentation

One of the most useful features of IEx is its ability to provide documentation for Elixir modules and functions via the h helper. For example:

```
iex(2)> h Enum.map
```

The above command retrieves and displays the documentation for the Enum.map/2 function. The documentation provides details on the function's purpose, usage, parameters, and examples.

Variable Persistence

Variables declared in IEx persist throughout the session, allowing you to reference them in subsequent commands. For instance:

```
iex(3)> name = "Elixir"
"Elixir"
iex(4)> IO.puts("Hello, #{name}!")
Hello, Elixir!
:ok
```

Here, the variable name is assigned the string "Elixir". This variable is then used within a string interpolation in the IO.puts/2 function.

Advanced IEx Features

IEx provides several advanced features that enhance the development workflow.

Autocompletion

IEx includes a built-in autocompletion mechanism. By pressing the Tab key, you can autocomplete module and function names. For example:

```
iex(5)> Enum.ma
map/2 map/3 map_every/3 map_join/2 map_join/3 map_reduce/3
iex(5)> Enum.map
```

This feature accelerates coding by reducing the need to type long module or function names completely.

Debugging with IEx

IEx enables basic debugging through the IEx.pry/1 function, which allows you to pause the execution of your code and inspect its current state. To use IEx.pry/1, you need to add a breakpoint in your code:

```
defmodule DebugExample do
  def hello(name) do
    IO.puts("Hello, #{name}!")
    IEx.pry()
  end
end
```

After running the above code, when the hello/1 function is invoked, execution will pause at IEx.pry/1, and you will be able to interact with the current binding:

```
iex(6)> DebugExample.hello("world")
Hello, world!
Request to pry #PID<0.109.0> at lib/debug_example.ex:3
Allow? [Yn] y
```

At this point, you can inspect the state of variables and even alter the control flow if necessary.

Using the .iex.exs Configuration File

IEx can be configured using the .iex.exs file. This file is loaded each time IEx starts, making it a useful place to define aliases, import common modules, or set up other configurations. For example, creating a .iex.exs file with:

```
\# .iex.exs
import Ecto.Query
alias MyApp.Repo
```

will ensure that the Ecto.Query module is imported and MyApp.Repo alias is available whenever you start IEx.

By leveraging the capabilities of IEx, including its real-time feedback, documentation access, autocompletion, and debugging tools, developers can significantly streamline the development process. The shell's interactive nature makes it an invaluable tool for experimenting with code snippets, learning new features, and diagnosing issues quickly.

1.4 Basic Syntax and Conventions

Elixir's syntax is influenced by Ruby and Erlang, aiming to offer expressiveness and clarity. It is crucial to understand the fundamental syntax and conventions to effectively write Elixir code. This section explores key constructs such as delimiters, modules, functions, pattern matching, and operators.

Elixir code files typically have an .ex or .exs extension:

- .ex files are compiled and produce .beam files executed on the BEAM virtual machine.
- .exs files are used for scripting; they are interpreted without generating bytecode.

Elixir Modules and Functions

Modules encapsulate functions and create namespaces to prevent name collisions. They are defined using the defmodule keyword:

```
defmodule Math do
  def add(a, b) do
    a + b
  end

  def subtract(a, b) do
    a - b
  end
end
```

Functions within modules are defined using the def keyword. By convention, function names are written in snake_case:

```
defmodule Greeter do
  def say_hello(name) do
    "Hello, #{name}!"
  end
end
```

Pattern Matching

Pattern matching is a powerful feature in Elixir, providing a mechanism to destructure data and control flow based on the shape of the data. The = operator in Elixir is not a traditional assignment operator but a match operator:

```
{x, y} = {1, 2} # x = 1, y = 2
```

Pattern matching also works within function definitions:

```
defmodule Math do
  def zero?(0), do: true
  def zero?(_), do: false
end
```

In this example, the zero?/1 function matches exactly on 0 for the first clause and uses the underscore _ to denote any other value in the second clause.

Control Flow

Elixir's primary control flow constructs include if, unless, case, cond, and with:

```
if x > 0 do
  "Positive"
else
  "Non-positive"
end
```

```
case {1, 2, 3} do
  {1, x, 3} -> "x = #{x}"
  _ -> "No match"
end
```

```
cond do
  x > 0 -> "Positive"
  x < 0 -> "Negative"
  true -> "Zero"
end
```

Operators

Elixir supports various operators for arithmetic, comparison, and logical operations. Here are some frequently used operators:

- Arithmetic: +, -, *, /
- Comparison: ==, !=, ===, <, <=, >, >=
- Boolean: and, or, not

The === operator is a strict comparison operator taking into account the type:

```
1 == 1.0 # true
1 === 1.0 # false
```

Pipe Operator

The pipe operator |> in Elixir allows for more readable and composable code by passing the result of one function as the first argument to the next function:

```
"elixir" |> String.upcase |> String.reverse
```

This chain transforms the string "elixir" to "RIXILE".

Identifiers and Naming Conventions

Elixir follows specific conventions for naming:

- Variable names should be written in snake_case (e.g., total_amount).
- Module names are written in PascalCase (e.g., MyModule).
- Constants and module attributes use the @ prefix (e.g., @version).

Adhering to these conventions ensures code readability and maintainability.

Here is an example module that follows these conventions:

```
defmodule Circle do
  @pi 3.14

  def area(radius) do
    @pi * radius * radius
  end
end
```

Comments

Comments in Elixir begin with the hash (#) symbol. Single-line comments are beneficial for clarifying code behavior:

```
# Calculate the area of a circle
defmodule Circle do
  def area(radius) do
    3.14 * radius * radius
  end
end
```

Mutex-free concurrency, its simplicity, and ease of adoption make Elixir syntax and conventions beneficial for both small scripts and large-scale applications.

1.5 Hello World in Elixir

To begin our exploration of Elixir programming, we will start with a simple example: printing "Hello, World!" to the console. This elementary program serves as a foundational step to familiarize ourselves with Elixir's syntax and execution model.

In Elixir, the standard way to output text to the console is by using the IO.puts/1 function. The IO module provides a variety of utilities for input and output operations, and puts is a commonly used function within this module to print a string followed by a newline.

Let us write our first Elixir script. Create a file named hello_world.exs. The .exs extension denotes an Elixir script file, which can be executed directly from the command line. Enter the following code into the file:

```
IO.puts("Hello, World!")
```

This single line of code invokes the IO.puts/1 function with the string "Hello, World!" as its argument.

To run the script, open a terminal and navigate to the directory containing the hello_world.exs file. Execute the script using the elixir command as follows:

```
$ elixir hello_world.exs
Hello, World!
```

Upon execution, you should see the output "Hello, World!" printed to the console, confirming that our Elixir environment is correctly set up and functioning.

Next, we will explore how to accomplish the same task within the Elixir interactive shell, known as IEx. The interactive shell allows for real-time code evaluation and is a powerful tool for experimenting with code snippets and testing functions. To start IEx, simply type iex in your terminal:

```
$ iex
Erlang/OTP 24 [erts-12.1.5] [source] [smp:4:4] [ds:4:4:10] [async-threads:1] [jit]
Interactive Elixir (1.12.2) - press Ctrl+C to exit (type h() ENTER for help)
iex(1)>
```

Once inside the IEx shell, you can execute Elixir code in real-time. Type the following command to print "Hello, World!" directly:

```
IO.puts("Hello, World!")
```

Pressing enter will result in the output:

```
Hello, World!
:ok
```

The :ok atom following the printed message signifies that the operation completed successfully. Atoms in Elixir are constants whose value is their own name. They are frequently used to signify the successful completion of functions and other control structures.

Between using script files and the interactive shell, we have demonstrated two fundamental ways to run Elixir code. Moving forward, we will delve deeper into understanding the context surrounding functions and modules. Elixir enforces modularity through the use of modules, which encapsulate related functions and provide structure to the codebase.

To illustrate this, let us refactor our "Hello, World!" example into a module. Create a new file named hello_world_module.exs and add the following code:

```
defmodule HelloWorld do
  def greet do
    IO.puts("Hello, World!")
  end
end

HelloWorld.greet()
```

In this example, we define a module named HelloWorld using the defmodule keyword. Within this module, we define a function named greet using the def keyword. The greet function, when called, will execute the IO.puts/1 command to print "Hello, World!" to the console.

To execute this module-based script, return to your terminal and run:

```
$ elixir hello_world_module.exs
Hello, World!
```

This modular approach exemplifies how Elixir encourages structured and reusable code.

Writing and organizing code into modules is a fundamental aspect of Elixir programming. As we progress through this book, we shall repeatedly see the use of modules to group and manage related functionalities effectively.

This initiation into Elixir programming, by way of a "Hello, World!" example, introduces us to essential concepts such as the interactive shell, basic I/O operations, and modular design. Armed with this knowledge, we are well-equipped to further investigate the capabilities and versatility of Elixir in subsequent chapters and sections.

1.6 Variables and Data Types Overview

In Elixir, as in many programming languages, variables and data types play a crucial role in the construction and manipulation of data. Understanding the mechanisms of variable assignment and the types of data that can be handled is foundational for building effective programs.

Variables in Elixir are bindings to values and can be reassigned but are immutable once defined, meaning that reassigning a variable creates a new binding rather than altering the existing one. Variable names are written in snake_case, a convention in which words are lowercase and separated by underscores.

```
name = "Elixir"
age = 10
pi = 3.14
```

In the example above, name, age, and pi are variables bound to a string, an integer, and a float, respectively. Variables in Elixir do not have fixed types; they carry the type of the value they are assigned.

Data Types in Elixir include common types such as integers, floats, booleans, atoms, tuples, lists, maps, and binaries. Each type has specific characteristics and use cases.

1. *Integers and Floats:* Numbers in Elixir can be integers or floats. Integers are written in standard form, while floats require a decimal point.

```
integer_value = 42
float_value = 3.14159
```

The integer_value is an integer, and the float_value is a floating-point number. Operations between these types are straightforward, but mixing them in arithmetic expressions may yield a float.

```
result1 = 1 + 2 # 3 (Integer)
result2 = 1.0 + 2 # 3.0 (Float)
```

Outputs:

```
result1 = 3
result2 = 3.0
```

2. Booleans: Elixir uses the boolean values true and false, which are essential for logical operations.

```
is_valid = true
is_empty = false
```

Booleans support logical operators such as and, or, and not.

```
is_valid and is_empty # false
is_valid or is_empty # true
not is_valid # false
```

3. Atoms: Atom literals are constants whose value is their name, often used to denote status, labels, or messages.

```
status = :ok
error_message = :error
```

Atoms are notable for their uniqueness and efficient comparison, making them useful in pattern matching and as labels for data.

4. Tuples: Tuples are ordered collections of fixed-size, usually used to group multiple pieces of data. They are declared with curly braces.

```
coordinates = {40.7128, -74.0060}
person = {"Alice", 30}
```

Tuples enable easy access to their elements by index positions.

```
first_element = elem(coordinates, 0) # 40.7128
second_element = elem(coordinates, 1) # -74.0060
```

elem/2 is an in-built function to retrieve tuple elements by position.

5. Lists: Lists are collections of variable length and are versatile for managing sequential data. Declared using square brackets, they can store different types of elements.

```
numbers = [1, 2, 3, 4, 5]
mixed_list = [42, "hello", :world, 3.14]
```

Operable using head-tail decomposition, lists can easily traverse, manipulate, and pattern match.

```
[head | tail] = mixed_list
# head = 42
# tail = ["hello", :world, 3.14]
```

6. *Maps:* Maps are key-value stores with arbitrary keys. They provide more flexibility than tuples for associative data.

```
user = %{"name" => "Bob", "age" => 25}
grades = %{:math => 95, :science => 88}
```

Keys can be accessed and modified using the Map module functions.

```
user_name = Map.get(user, "name") # "Bob"
updated_user = Map.put(user, "age", 26)
```

7. *Binaries:* Binaries represent sequences of bytes, used in processing raw byte data and strings.

```
binary_data = <<1, 2, 3, 4>>
string = "hello"
binary_string = :binary.bin_to_list(string)
```

It is vital to understand these types and their representations for effective data manipulation and storage in Elixir. Transitioning between and operating with different data types are cornerstones of building robust and efficient Elixir applications. The use of atoms for constant identifiers, lists for sequential collections, and maps for key-value associations exemplifies the flexible yet powerful nature of data handling within Elixir.

1.7 Comments and Documentation

In software development, comments and documentation are pivotal for maintaining code readability and understanding, especially when working in teams or maintaining projects over long periods. Elixir provides robust support for both inline comments and comprehensive documentation, making it an exemplary tool for these purposes.

Comments in Elixir begin with the % character and extend to the end of the line. These comments are entirely ignored by the Elixir compiler, serving purely as annotations for developers.

```
# This is a single-line comment in Elixir
result = Enum.sum([1, 2, 3, 4, 5]) # Enum.sum calculates the sum of the list elements
```

For more extensive commentary, Elixir does not natively support multi-line comments, but it is common to use consecutive single-line comments to adhere to this requirement:

```
# This function calculates the factorial of a given number.
# It uses pattern matching and recursion to achieve the result.
defmodule Math do
  def factorial(0), do: 1
  def factorial(n) when n > 0 do
    n * factorial(n-1)
  end
end
```

Elixir documentation is more structured and goes beyond simple comments. It employs a sophisticated system known as Doc, which allows embedding documentation directly within the source code. This embedded documentation is accessible both within the codebase and through external tools.

To create documentation in Elixir, we use triple-double-quote "\"\"\" delimited docstrings. These docstrings can be assigned at multiple levels: module, function, or macro.

Module Documentation

Module-level documentation provides a high-level overview of the module's purpose and functionality. It is typically placed at the top of the module.

```
defmodule Math do
  @moduledoc """
  The Math module provides basic arithmetic functions including
  addition, subtraction, multiplication, and division.
  """
  ...
end
```

In this example, @moduledoc is used to describe the purpose of the Math module. This information can then be accessed via documentation tools or directly from the IEx shell.

Function and Macro Documentation

Function and macro-level documentation is specific to individual functions or macros within the module. @doc is used for this purpose and should precede the documented function or macro.

```
defmodule Math do
  @moduledoc """
  The Math module provides basic arithmetic functions.
  """

  @doc """
```

```
  Calculates the factorial of a non-negative integer.

  ## Parameters

    - n: A non-negative integer.

  ## Examples

      iex> Math.factorial(5)
      120

  """
  def factorial(0), do: 1
  def factorial(n) when n > 0 do
    n * factorial(n-1)
  end
end
```

Here, @doc is followed by a string detailing the function factorial/1, including parameters, explanations, and examples. The ## markers help format the documentation into sections such as Parameters and Examples, promoting clarity and structure.

Retrieving Documentation

Elixir's iex shell provides a convenient means to access module and function documentation. By invoking the h helper followed by the module or function name, the corresponding documentation is retrieved.

```
iex> h Math
iex> h Math.factorial
```

The above commands will display the documentation for the Math module and its function factorial/1, respectively, facilitating an interactive exploration of the documented code.

Creating Documentation with ExDoc

ExDoc, an official Elixir project, enables the generation of HTML and EPUB documentation from annotated code. To use ExDoc, add it to your project's dependencies within the mix.exs file:

```
defp deps do
  [
    {:ex_doc, "~> 0.24", only: :dev, runtime: false}
  ]
end
```

Run mix deps.get to install the new dependency. Thereafter, you can generate documentation by executing the command mix docs. This produces a directory doc/ containing HTML files viewable in a web browser.

```
$ mix docs
```

Proper commenting and documentation are invaluable practices in software engineering. Elixir's robust system supports these practices, making it easier to write understandable, maintainable, and well-documented code.

1.8 Elixir Tooling and Ecosystem

Elixir offers a robust ecosystem and an array of tools designed to enhance the development process, streamline deployment, and ensure high performance. This section delves into some of the critical tools and libraries that are indispensable for any Elixir developer, elucidating their purpose and usage while integrating them into your workflow.

Mix Mix is an essential build tool that comes pre-installed with Elixir. It serves multiple purposes, including project management, compilation, testing, and dependency management. Here is an example of creating a new project using Mix:

```
$ mix new my_project
* creating README.md
* creating .formatter.exs
* creating .gitignore
* creating mix.exs
* creating config
* creating config/config.exs
* creating lib
* creating lib/my_project.ex
* creating test
* creating test/test_helper.exs
* creating test/my_project_test.exs
```

Mix also facilitates running tasks like compilations and tests:

```
$ cd my_project
$ mix compile
$ mix test
```

Hex Hex is the package manager for the Elixir ecosystem, akin to npm for JavaScript or pip for Python. It allows developers to fetch, publish, and manage dependencies. To include a library in your project, you first add it to your mix.exs file under the deps function:

```
defp deps do
  [
    {:ecto, "~> 3.0"}
  ]
end
```

You then run the following commands to install the dependency:

```
$ mix deps.get
```

ExUnit ExUnit is Elixir's built-in testing framework, designed for unit and integration testing. It is automatically included in new projects created with Mix. A basic test file for a module may look like this:

```
defmodule MyProjectTest do
  use ExUnit.Case
  doctest MyProject

  test "the truth" do
    assert 1 + 1 == 2
  end
end
```

To execute tests, simply run:

```
$ mix test
```

```
Finished in 0.03 seconds
1 test, 0 failures
```

Dialyzer Dialyzer is a static analysis tool for Erlang, and by extension, Elixir, used to find bugs such as type errors, dead code, and other discrepancies. To use Dialyzer, you need to add it as a dependency in your mix.exs:

```
defp deps do
  [
    {:dialyxir, "~> 1.0", only: [:dev], runtime: false}
  ]
end
```

Fetch and compile the dependency:

```
$ mix deps.get
$ mix deps.compile
```

You generate a PLT (Persistent Lookup Table) for your project and dependencies:

```
$ mix dialyzer --build
```

Finally, run Dialyzer:

```
$ mix dialyzer
```

Credo Credo is a static code analysis tool focusing on code consistency and best practices. It helps maintain a clean codebase by providing suggestions and warnings. Add Credo to your project's dependencies:

```
defp deps do
  [
    {:credo, "~> 1.6", only: [:dev, :test], runtime: false}
  ]
end
```

After fetching the dependency, you can start using Credo:

```
$ mix credo
```

```
Consistency

[C]  Module attribute @moduledoc is missing.
     lib/my_project.ex:1
```

Phoenix Framework Phoenix is a web development framework for Elixir that offers high performance and productivity. It is used for building real-time applications with Channels, a mechanism for handling WebSockets. To create a new Phoenix project:

```
$ mix archive.install hex phx_new
$ mix phx.new my_app
```

Navigate to your newly generated project directory and start the server:

```
$ cd my_app
$ mix phx.server
```

Your application will be accessible at http://localhost:4000.

Observer Observer is a graphical frontend for visualizing the Erlang runtime. It offers tools to monitor processes, applications, memory, and more. First, you need to ensure that the observer application is running:

```
:observer.start()
```

A window will appear displaying various tabs that provide insights into system performance and resource utilization.

Distillery Distillery is used for building and deploying Elixir applications. It helps create releases that are self-contained and easy to deploy. To get started, add Distillery to your dependency list:

```
defp deps do
  [
    {:distillery, "~> 2.1", runtime: false}
  ]
end
```

Generate release files:

```
$ mix release.init
```

Then build a release:

```
$ mix release
```

This will create a self-contained bundle in the _build directory, suitable for deployment to production environments.

Together, these tools and the Elixir ecosystem offer a comprehensive toolkit that developers can leverage to maximize productivity and maintain code quality. Integrating these tools into your development pipeline will greatly aid in creating robust, maintainable Elixir applications.

Chapter 2

Basic Data Types and Structures

This chapter delves into the fundamental data types and structures in Elixir, including atoms, strings, numbers, booleans, lists, and tuples. It explains how to use maps, keyword lists, binaries, charlists, and bitstrings. Additionally, the chapter covers nested data structures and emphasizes the importance of immutability in Elixir, providing a comprehensive understanding of the building blocks necessary for effective programming in the language.

2.1 Atoms and Strings

Atoms and strings are two fundamental data types in Elixir, both of which are used extensively in the language for a variety of purposes. Understanding their properties, the ways in which they are used, and their interactions with other data types is essential for writing effective Elixir programs.

Atoms are constants whose values are their own name. They are used to denote fixed values and are often employed for expressing keys in maps, message tags, and state names in state machines, among other applications. Atoms are preceded by a colon (:) and can contain letters, digits, underscores, and at-signs (@). For example, the following snippet shows a few atoms in use:

```
:name
:ok
:error
:user_123
:email_sent
@user_registered
```

Atoms are used because they provide a unique and clear identifier which is both concise and readable. The fact that atoms' values are their own names allows for human-readable code that retains clarity and purpose.

An important characteristic of atoms in Elixir is that they are not garbage collected. Therefore, excessive use of atoms, especially with dynamically generated names, can lead to performance issues and should be used judiciously.

Strings in Elixir are UTF-8 encoded binaries, encapsulated within double quotes ("). Strings can contain any sequence of characters, including letters, digits, spaces, special characters, and escape sequences. Here are a few examples of string usage:

```
"Hello, World!"
"Elixir is a dynamic, functional language."
"Let's write some \n Elixir code!"
"The value is: #{value}"
```

Elixir provides a comprehensive set of functions for manipulating strings through the String module. For example, to concatenate two strings, you can use the String.concat/2 function or the <> operator. Here are both methods illustrated:

```
string1 = "Hello"
string2 = "World"

concatenated = String.concat(string1, " ", string2)
concatenated = string1 <> " " <> string2
```

Elixir strings can be dynamically interpolated using the #{} syntax. This is particularly useful for embedding variable values or expressions within strings:

```
name = "Alice"
greeting = "Hello, #{name}!"
IO.puts greeting
```

```
Hello, Alice!
```

When using strings as keys in maps, it is essential to distinguish them from atoms. Strings and atoms, though similar in purpose when used as keys, have different memory and performance characteristics. For example:

```
%{"name" => "Alice", "age" => 30}
%{name: "Bob", age: 25}
```

In the first map, "name" and "age" are string keys, whereas in the second map, name and age are atom keys. Both are valid but serve different use cases based on the persistence and uniqueness requirements of the key values.

Atoms in Elixir can be compared using the standard comparison operators, which compares atoms lexicographically. For example:

```
IO.puts :a < :b
IO.puts :hello == :world
```

```
true
false
```

In general, both atoms and strings are also used heavily in pattern matching. Atoms often serve as tag identifiers in complex data structures, while strings can be matched directly:

```
case some_value do
  :ok -> IO.puts "Operation succeeded"
  :error -> IO.puts "Operation failed"
  _ -> IO.puts "Unknown status"
end

case some_string do
  "open" -> IO.puts "Resource is open"
  "closed" -> IO.puts "Resource is closed"
  _ -> IO.puts "Unknown resource state"
end
```

By understanding the nuances of atoms and strings, Elixir developers can make informed choices, improving code clarity, performance, and overall robustness. This section provides a bedrock upon which more complex data structures and operations can be understood in subsequent sections.

2.2 Numbers and Arithmetic

Elixir provides comprehensive support for numerical data types and arithmetic operations, which are essential in many programming tasks. Elixir's number types fall primarily into two categories: integers and floating-point numbers.

Elixir integers are sequences of digits without a decimal point, fitting within the range of a 64-bit signed integer. They can be positive, negative, or zero. Below is an example of assigning and using integers in Elixir:

```
int1 = 42
int2 = -7
```

In this example, int1 is assigned a value of 42, and int2 is assigned a value of -7. Elixir can handle very large integers due to arbitrary precision arithmetic, making it suitable for applications that require large computations.

Floating-point numbers in Elixir are also known as floats and include a decimal point. They adhere to the IEEE 754 standard for double-precision floating-point arithmetic. Here's an example of using floating-point numbers:

```
float1 = 3.14
float2 = -2.5
```

In this case, float1 holds the value 3.14, and float2 holds the value -2.5. When working with floats, be aware of potential precision issues due to the inherent limitations of floating-point representation.

Elixir permits implicit conversion between integers and floats in arithmetic calculations. This feature allows for intuitive handling of mixed-number operations without requiring explicit type casts. Consider the following examples:

```
result1 = 5 + 3.2 # Integer and float addition
result2 = 10 / 2 # Integer division resulting in a float
result3 = 7 * 1.5 # Integer and float multiplication
```

Here, result1 will be 8.2 (a float), result2 will be 5.0 (a float), and result3 will be 10.5 (a float).

Elixir supports standard arithmetic operations, including addition (+), subtraction (-), multiplication (*), and division (/). The division operation always yields a float. For integer division, Elixir uses the div function, while the rem function returns the remainder of an integer division. Examples of these functions are given below:

```
integer_division = div(10, 3) # Returns 3
remainder = rem(10, 3) # Returns 1
```

integer_division will be 3, which is the integer quotient of 10 divided by 3. remainder will be 1, which is the remainder.

Exponentiation in Elixir is performed using the :math.pow/2 function, which is part of the :math module. For instance:

```
power = :math.pow(2, 3) # Returns 8.0
```

The result here, power, is 8.0, calculated as 2 raised to the power of 3.

Elixir also includes a variety of mathematical functions through the :math module, such as logarithms (:math.log/1), square roots (:math.sqrt/1), and trigonometric functions (:math.sin/1, :math.cos/1, etc.). Some examples include:

```
log_value = :math.log(10) # Natural logarithm of 10
sqrt_value = :math.sqrt(16) # Square root of 16
sin_value = :math.sin(:math.pi) # Sine of pi
```

Here, log_value will be approximately 2.3026, sqrt_value will be 4.0, and sin_value will be a very small number close to 0.

When handling monetary values or other cases requiring exact decimal representation, consider using libraries such as Decimal, which provides arbitrary precision floating-point decimal arithmetic.

In Elixir, the immutability of data extends to numbers. Any assignment to a variable always creates a new variable; altering a number's value is effectively assigning a new value to a new variable, maintaining the original value unaltered. This attribute is crucial for ensuring predictability and thread safety in concurrent programming.

Addresses common pitfalls when working with numbers in Elixir. One should be cautious about using floating-point numbers for comparisons and aware of the precision limitations. Utilizing functions like Kernel.==/2 or employing custom comparison functions can help manage these issues effectively.

These features make Elixir's arithmetic and number handling robust and reliable, providing the foundational support necessary for diverse programming challenges. This consistency in numerical operations ensures that programs can handle small-scale calculations and large-scale computations with equal ease.

2.3 Booleans and Comparison Operators

In Elixir, booleans are a fundamental data type that represents two possible values: true and false. These values are essential for controlling the flow of logic within a program through conditional statements and loops. Understanding how to use boolean values effectively and the various comparison operators available in Elixir is crucial for writing robust and error-free code.

Boolean Values

Elixir provides two literals for boolean values:

- true
- false

These literals can be used directly in expressions, and their primary function is to control the logic of the program.

Comparison Operators

Comparison operators in Elixir are used to compare two values and return a boolean result. Elixir supports standard comparison operators such as ==, !=, <, <=, >, and >=. These operators can be applied to numbers, strings, and other comparable data types.

```
iex> 5 == 5
true
iex> 5 != 10
true
iex> 5 < 10
true
iex> 5 <= 5
true
iex> 10 > 5
true
iex> 10 >= 5
true
```

It is crucial to note that Elixir distinguishes between the strict equality operator === and the relaxed equality operator ==. The strict equality operator takes into account the type of the operands, whereas the relaxed equality operator does not. This distinction is particularly important in dynamically-typed languages like Elixir.

```
iex> 5 == 5.0
true
iex> 5 === 5.0
false
```

Logical Operators

Elixir also provides logical operators that are used to combine boolean values. The primary logical operators include and, or, and not.

- The and operator returns true if both operands are true, otherwise it returns false.
- The or operator returns true if at least one of the operands is true, otherwise it returns false.
- The not operator returns the opposite boolean value of its operand.

```
iex> true and false
false
iex> true or false
true
iex> not true
false
```

It is important to understand the short-circuit behavior of logical operators in Elixir. The and and or operators are short-circuit operators, meaning they may not evaluate the second operand if the result can already be determined by the first operand.

```
iex> false and (IO.puts("This will not be printed") == :ok)
false
iex> true or (IO.puts("This will not be printed") == :ok)
true
```

Combined Usage in Conditional Structures

Boolean values and comparison operators are frequently used together within conditional structures to control the flow of the program. Elixir provides if and unless constructs for such purposes.

```
if 10 > 5 do
  IO.puts("10 is greater than 5")
end

unless 5 > 10 do
  IO.puts("5 is not greater than 10")
end
```

These constructs are evaluated based on the result of the boolean expression. If the expression in the if construct evaluates to true, the block of code within the do block is executed. Similarly, the unless construct executes the block of code within the do block if the boolean expression evaluates to false.

Boolean values and comparison operators form the basis of logical decision-making in Elixir programs. Mastering their usage paves the way for writing expressive, clear, and correct Elixir code.

2.4 Lists and Tuples

Lists and tuples are fundamental data structures in Elixir that allow efficient grouping and manipulation of elements. These data structures play crucial roles in various programming tasks, providing distinct semantics and performance characteristics.

Lists in Elixir are collections of elements, which can include any kind of data type. They are implemented as linked lists, meaning each element points to the next, making prepend operations fast. Lists are created using square brackets, with elements separated by commas.

Tuples, on the other hand, are fixed-size collections of elements, implemented as contiguous memory blocks. Tuples are constant in size and use parentheses with elements separated by commas. Tuples enable fast access to elements by index but are generally more costly to modify since modifying a tuple generates a new tuple.

```
# Example of a list
list = [1, 2, 3, 4, 5]

# Example of a tuple
tuple = {:ok, "Hello", 42}
```

To understand the structural and operational differences, consider the following operations on lists and tuples:

Lists support the following basic operations:

- Accessing elements
- Adding elements
- Concatenating lists
- Subtracting elements
- Head and tail operations

Accessing elements of a list is not a direct operation since it traverses the list until the specified position. To illustrate:

```
# Fetching the third element (note: lists are zero-indexed)
Enum.at(list, 2) # => 3
```

Adding elements is straightforward:

```
# Prepending an element (fast operation)
new_list = [0 | list] # => [0, 1, 2, 3, 4, 5]

# Appending an element (more costly)
new_list = list ++ [6] # => [1, 2, 3, 4, 5, 6]
```

Tuples support the following operations:

- Accessing elements by index
- Retrieving the size
- Modifying elements (results in a new tuple)

Accessing elements of a tuple is direct and efficient:

```
# Fetching the second element
elem(tuple, 1) # => "Hello"
```

Retrieving the size of a tuple and modifying elements requires:

```
# Getting the size
tuple_size(tuple) # => 3

# Modifying an element (generates a new tuple)
new_tuple = put_elem(tuple, 2, 43) # => {:ok, "Hello", 43}
```

While lists are most commonly used due to their flexibility and convenience in Elixir, tuples are preferred when the fixed structure is known at compile-time or when constant time access to elements is required. The choice between lists and tuples significantly impacts performance and use-case suitability.

When dealing with nested data structures, lists and tuples can be combined:

```
# A list of tuples
list_of_tuples = [{:ok, 1}, {:error, 2}, {:ok, 3}]

# A tuple containing lists
tuple_with_lists = {[:a, :b, :c], [:x, :y, :z]}
```

Exploring list-specific functions through the Enum and List modules and tuple-specific functions through the Kernel module provides deeper understanding and utility:

```
# Enum: map function - applies the given function to each item
Enum.map(list, fn x -> x * 2 end) # => [2, 4, 6, 8, 10]

# List: delete function - removes the specified item
List.delete(list, 3) # => [1, 2, 4, 5]

# Tuple: tuple_size function - returns the number of elements
tuple_size(tuple) # => 3

# Kernel: elem function - retrieves element by index
elem(tuple, 1) # => "Hello"
```

Understanding both lists and tuples is crucial for efficient programming in Elixir. These structures enable managing collections of data with varying performance characteristics and use-cases, encouraging thoughtful selection of the appropriate data structure based on the requirements.

2.5 Maps and Keyword Lists

Maps and keyword lists are essential data structures in Elixir, providing flexibility for storing key-value pairs. Maps offer a robust solution for managing collections of data, while keyword lists serve as an ordered collection with slightly different characteristics. Understanding these structures is crucial for efficient data handling and manipulation in Elixir.

Maps in Elixir are created using the % syntax. Each key in a map can be any Elixir term, and the map itself is unordered, allowing for average time complexity of $O(1)$ for insertions and lookups. Here is an example of creating and accessing maps:

```
# Creating a map
student_grades = %{"Alice" => "A", "Bob" => "B", "Cathy" => "B+"}

# Accessing values using keys
grade_alice = student_grades["Alice"]
IO.puts grade_alice
```

```
A
```

Maps can also be created using atoms as keys, which can be more concise and readable:

```
info = %{name: "Alice", age: 25, city: "New York"}

# Accessing values using atom keys
name = info[:name]
IO.puts name
```

Alice

Updating maps in Elixir leverages the use of the | operator to create a new map with the updated value, maintaining immutability:

```
# Updating a map
info = %{info | city: "San Francisco"}
IO.inspect info
```

%{age: 25, city: "San Francisco", name: "Alice"}

Keyword lists, on the other hand, are lists of two-element tuples where the first element is an atom. They maintain the order of elements and allow duplicate keys, which makes them suitable for options passed to functions. Here is an example of a keyword list:

```
# Creating a keyword list
options = [name: "Bob", age: 30, city: "Boston"]

# Accessing values
IO.inspect Keyword.get(options, :age)
```

30

Unlike maps, keyword lists are simply lists under the hood, thus lookups have a time complexity of $O(n)$. Keyword lists can be particularly useful in defining function options due to their readability and ordered nature:

```
# Function with keyword list arguments
defmodule Greeting do
  def greet(name, opts \\ []) do
    greeting = Keyword.get(opts, :greeting, "Hello")
    IO.puts "#{greeting}, #{name}!"
  end
end

Greeting.greet("Alice", greeting: "Hi")
```

Hi, Alice!

Despite their similarities, maps and keyword lists serve different use cases. Maps are preferable for large, unordered collections of key-value pairs where fast access is crucial. Keyword lists, in contrast, are more suitable for representing options and configurations due to their ordered and lightweight nature.

Transitioning smoothly from keyword lists to maps or vice versa can sometimes be necessary. Elixir provides mechanisms to facilitate this conversion. Here is how to convert a keyword list to a map and vice versa:

```
# Keyword list to map
options = [name: "Charlie", age: 28]
```

```
map_options = Enum.into(options, %{})
IO.inspect map_options

# Map to keyword list
map_data = %{job: "Engineer", location: "California"}
keyword_data = Enum.into(map_data, [])
IO.inspect keyword_data
```

```
%{age: 28, name: "Charlie"}
[job: "Engineer", location: "California"]
```

Maps and keyword lists enable developers to choose the most efficient and readable structures for varying scenarios in Elixir, ensuring clear and maintainable codebases.

2.6 Binaries, charlists, and bitstrings

Elixir provides robust support for binary data, charlists, and bitstrings, which are essential for handling raw data and interfacing with external systems. Understanding these data types is crucial for efficient data manipulation and transformation.

Binaries are used to handle sequences of bytes. In Elixir, binaries are enclosed in double quotes. They are often used for string manipulation and other operations where byte-level data handling is necessary. A binary can be created and manipulated as shown in the following examples:

```
iex> binary = "hello"
"hello"
iex> byte_size(binary)
5
iex> <<104, 101, 108, 108, 111>> = binary
"hello"
```

In the example above, the byte_size/1 function returns the number of bytes in the binary. The binary pattern matching syntax, «...», is utilized for matching and constructing binaries from their byte components.

Charlists are simply lists of characters, where each character is represented by its ASCII value. Unlike binaries, which are enclosed in double quotes, charlists are enclosed in single quotes:

```
iex> charlist = 'hello'
'hello'
iex> Enum.map(charlist, fn char -> char + 1 end)
'ifmmp'
```

Charlists are useful in certain scenarios, particularly when interfacing with Erlang libraries that expect charlists instead of binaries. The example demonstrates a simple transformation of each character in the charlist using the Enum.map/2 function, incrementing the ASCII value of each character by 1.

In Elixir, both binaries and charlists can be converted between each other:

```
iex> binary = "hello"
"hello"
iex> charlist = to_charlist(binary)
'hello'
iex> binary_again = to_string(charlist)
"hello"
```

The to_charlist/1 function converts a binary to a charlist, and to_string/1 converts a charlist back to a binary. These conversions are often necessary when working with different libraries or parts of a system that expect specific data representations.

Bitstrings are a more generalized form of binaries and can represent sequences of bits that do not necessarily form complete bytes. Bitstrings are defined using the same «» syntax but can include a bit size specification. This allows representation and manipulation of nonstandard data sizes:

```
iex> bitstring = <<1 :: size(1), 0 :: size(1), 1 :: size(1)>>
<<5::3>>
iex> bit_size(bitstring)
3
iex> byte_size(bitstring)
1
```

In this example, a bitstring of size 3 bits is created, and the bit_size/1 function confirms its bit size. The byte_size/1 function, however, returns the number of bytes that the bitstring occupies, which is 1 byte in this case, despite only 3 bits being used.

Bitstrings are especially powerful when combined with pattern matching. This allows the deconstruction of packed formats and protocols efficiently. Consider parsing a binary where the first 3 bits represent a header and the next 5 bits represent a value:

```
iex> <<header :: size(3), value :: size(5)>> = <<29>>
<<29>>
iex> header
3
iex> value
5
```

Here, the binary «29» is parsed into a header and value, showcasing the utility of bitstring pattern matching.

When handling large data sets, interconverting between binaries, charlists, and bitstrings efficiently is pivotal. For instance, working with files in binary mode often entails reading data as binaries but converting them to charlists for processing:

```
iex> File.write!("example.bin", "Elixir binary data")
:ok
iex> {:ok, binary_data} = File.read("example.bin")
{:ok, "Elixir binary data"}
iex> charlist_data = to_charlist(binary_data)
'Elixir binary data'
iex> byte_size(binary_data)
19
iex> length(charlist_data)
19
```

This practical example highlights reading from a file into a binary, converting that binary data into a charlist, and verifying the data's size. Understanding these nuances ensures that one can handle different forms of data representation in a coherent and efficient manner.

Overall, the power and flexibility that Elixir provides for handling binaries, charlists, and bitstrings facilitate robust data manipulation capabilities, crucial for building efficient and reliable applications. Proper understanding and application of these data types make interfacing with binary protocols, manipulating textual data, and performing low-level data operations both straightforward and effective.

2.7 Nested Data Structures

In Elixir, nested data structures are widely used due to their expressiveness and utility in handling complex data. Nested data structures are collections that contain other collections, which can include lists, tuples, maps, and keyword lists inside each other. This section elaborates on the usage and manipulation of these nested constructs with appropriate examples to illustrate their functionality.

Consider a nested list, which is a list where each element could potentially be another list. Creating nested lists in Elixir is straightforward:

```
nested_list = [[1, 2, 3], [4, 5, 6], [7, 8, 9]]
```

To access elements within these nested lists, you can use the Enum module functions or direct indexing. For instance, to access the number 5 in the nested_list:

```
list_element = Enum.at(Enum.at(nested_list, 1), 1)
IO.puts(list_element) % This will output: 5
```

When working with nested tuples, similar principles apply, but tuples are accessed using pattern matching owing to their immutable and fixed-size properties. An example of a nested tuple:

```
nested_tuple = {:ok, {:data, 123, {1, 2, 3}}}
```

To extract the innermost tuple:

```
{:ok, {:data, _value, inner_tuple}} = nested_tuple
IO.inspect(inner_tuple) % This will output: {1, 2, 3}
```

Maps can also be nested. Consider the following structure:

```
nested_map = %{
  user: %{
    name: "Alice",
    settings: %{
      theme: "dark",
      notifications: true
    }
  }
}
```

Accessing elements within nested maps can be achieved using the Map.get/2 function or the dot syntax for more readability:

```
theme = nested_map[:user][:settings][:theme]
IO.puts(theme) % This will output: dark
```

Additions and updates within nested structures require special handling to maintain their immutability. The put_in/2 and update_in/3 functions from the Kernel module are used extensively with nested data. These functions accept a path to the data field and alter it accordingly:

```
updated_map = put_in(nested_map[:user][:settings][:theme], "light")
IO.inspect(updated_map)
```

Whereas put_in/2 modifies or inserts a value irrespective of its presence, update_in/3 allows for conditional updates:

```
updated_map = update_in(nested_map[:user][:settings][:notifications], &!&1)
IO.inspect(updated_map)
```

For operations requiring traversal and transformation of nested structures, the Enum and Kernel modules provide higher-order functions. An example application could be summing up all numerical values within a nested list:

```
defmodule NestedListHelper do
  def sum_nested_list(nested_list) do
    nested_list
    |> Enum.flat_map(& &1)
    |> Enum.sum()
  end
end

nested_list = [[1, 2, 3], [4, 5, 6], [7, 8, 9]]
total_sum = NestedListHelper.sum_nested_list(nested_list)
IO.puts(total_sum) % This will output: 45
```

Elixir's powerful pattern matching and enumerable capabilities make it efficient to navigate and manipulate highly nested structures. Ensuring immutability through data transformations maintains the integrity of these operations and aligns with Elixir's principles. Thus, effective handling of nested data is integral for complex, reliable, and scalable Elixir applications.

2.8 Immutability in Elixir

Immutability is a fundamental concept in Elixir and many modern functional programming languages. In Elixir, once a variable is bound to a value, that binding cannot be altered. This contrasts with imperative programming languages, where variables can be modified after their initial assignment. Embracing immutability provides several advantages, particularly in the realms of concurrent and parallel programming, as well as in maintaining the integrity and predictability of code.

To illustrate this, consider the following example:

```
x = 10
y = x + 5
```

Here, x is bound to the value 10, and y is bound to the result of adding 5 to x, producing 15. In this scenario, x retains its original value of 10, ensuring that every future reference to x will consistently yield 10.

Attempting to modify x directly would result in a rebinding rather than a mutation:

```
x = 10
x = 20
```

In this case, the second $x = 20$ simply rebinds x in the current scope to a new value of 20. The original binding of x to 10 is not altered but rather shadowed by the new binding within that scope.

This behavior ensures that data structures in Elixir are persistent. When manipulating these structures, new versions are created while the original remains unchanged. As a result, sharing and transferring data between different parts of a program becomes safer and free from unintended side effects.

Consider the example of modifying a list:

```
original_list = [1, 2, 3]
new_list = [0 | original_list]
```

In the above snippet, original_list remains [1, 2, 3] while new_list becomes [0, 1, 2, 3]. This demonstrates the creation of a new list without altering the original one.

Immutability also greatly simplifies reasoning about code, which is crucial for concurrent programming. Since values cannot change, shared state is not an issue. For instance, when running code on multiple processors, the same data can be accessed safely without race conditions or locks. This leads to more predictable and less error-prone programs.

To better understand how immutability is leveraged in Elixir's concurrency model, consider a simple example using the spawn/1 function to create a process:

```
defmodule Counter do
  def start(initial_count) do
    spawn(fn -> loop(initial_count) end)
  end

  defp loop(count) do
    receive do
      {:increment, caller} ->
        send(caller, {:new_count, count + 1})
        loop(count + 1)
    end
  end
end
```

Here, the Counter module defines a process that maintains an internal count. Each time an :increment message is received, the count is incremented, and a new count is sent back to the caller. Notice that the process retains state across messages by recursively calling loop/1 with an updated count. The previous count remains untouched, adhering to the principles of immutability.

Another illustrative scenario is the usage of maps in immutable contexts. Consider the following sequence:

```
map = %{"a" => 1, "b" => 2}
new_map = Map.put(map, "c", 3)
```

In this example, map is initially bound to a map with keys "a" and "b". The Map.put/3 function returns a new map new_map containing the original key-value pairs and an additional key "c" with value 3. The original map remains unchanged.

In practice, working with immutable data structures can often involve transformations and assertions without side effects. For instance, functions that process data can be composed fluently and checked robustly against expected outcomes. These operations facilitate reliable and maintainable software development by preventing inadvertent state changes.

Additionally, immutability complements Elixir's robust pattern matching capabilities, as the predictable nature of immutable values allows matches to be made against known and constant data structures. Consider an example with tuples:

```
case {:ok, 42} do
  {:ok, value} -> "The value is #{value}"
  {:error, _} -> "An error occurred"
end
```

Since the tuple (:ok, 42) does not change, the pattern match against (:ok, value) is guaranteed to succeed consistently, yielding reliable code execution paths.

Immutability in Elixir fosters a disciplined approach to programming, making it easier to write concurrent, scalable, and maintainable software. Understanding and embracing this concept is essential for leveraging the full potential of the language.

Chapter 3

Pattern Matching and Control Structures

This chapter explores pattern matching, a core feature of Elixir, demonstrating its use with basic data types, lists, and tuples, as well as in function definitions. It also introduces various control structures, including if, unless, case, cond, and with, along with error handling mechanisms such as try, rescue, and catch. The chapter further discusses the use of guards in function clauses, providing a solid foundation for writing concise and robust Elixir code.

3.1 Introduction to Pattern Matching

Pattern matching is a fundamental concept in Elixir that allows developers to bind variables to values or to check the structure and content of data. This feature makes the Elixir language more expressive and facilitates writing more readable and maintainable code. Understanding and effectively using pattern matching is crucial for mastering Elixir programming.

In Elixir, the match_operator = is employed for pattern matching. Fundamentally, it attempts to match the right-hand side of the operator to the left-hand side. If the match is successful, variables on the left-hand side are bound to corresponding values on the right-hand side. If the match fails, an error is raised. The most basic form of pattern matching involves simple data types:

```
x = 1
```

In this example, x is bound to the value 1. If x already holds a value, Elixir will rebind it. This rebinding characteristic distinguishes Elixir from many other programming languages where variables are immutable after their initial binding.

Pattern matching is not solely limited to numeric or simple data types; it extends to more complex types like tuples and lists. For instance:

```
{a, b, c} = {1, 2, 3}
```

Here, a, b, and c are bound to 1, 2, and 3, respectively. This method can be used to destructure tuples easily. Similarly, list pattern matching can bind elements of a list to variables:

```
[first | rest] = [1, 2, 3]
```

In this example, first gets bound to 1 and rest gets bound to [2, 3]. The | operator, known as the cons operator, divides the head of the list from its tail.

Pin Operator

The pin operator (^) allows pattern matching to be used with previously bound variables, enforcing their current values. This operator is useful when you wish to match against an existing value without rebinding it. Consider the following:

```
x = 1
^x = 1
```

In this snippet, the pattern match succeeds because x is pinned to its current value, which aligns with 1. If the value on the right-hand side does not match the pinned value of x, an error is thrown:

```
^x = 2
** (MatchError) no match of right hand side value: 2
```

Pattern Matching and Function Clauses

Pattern matching finds extensive use in defining function clauses in Elixir, making functions more robust and expressive. When a function is invoked, Elixir attempts to match the function arguments to the respective function clause. A successful match directs the program flow to the corresponding function body. This feature enables the creation of multiple function definitions with varying argument patterns.

```
defmodule Example do
  def greet({:person, name}) do
    "Hello, #{name}!"
  end

  def greet({:machine, id}) do
    "Greetings, machine numbered #{id}."
  end
end
```

In the Example module, the greet/1 function handles two different argument structures. The first clause matches a tuple formatted as {:person, name}, while the second clause matches a tuple formatted as {:machine, id}. When invoking Example.greet/1, Elixir determines the appropriate clause to execute based on the structure of the argument. For instance:

```
Example.greet({:person, "Alice"})
"Hello, Alice!"
Example.greet({:machine, 12345})
"Greetings, machine numbered 12345."
```

This ability to match on various patterns allows for writing polymorphic functions without resorting to a multitude of conditional statements.

By integrating pattern matching into function definitions and variable assignments, Elixir offers a powerful means to write clean, declarative, and efficient code.

3.2 Pattern Matching with Basic Data Types

Pattern matching is a fundamental feature in Elixir that allows the deconstruction of data structures and binding their contents to variables. This core mechanism permits sophisticated manipulations and assertions of data shape under specific contexts.

Elixir relies on the = operator for pattern matching. To understand its function, it is critical to note that this operator is not an assignment operator as in many other programming languages. Instead, it is a matching operator that attempts to match the term on the left-hand side (LHS) with the term on the right-hand side (RHS). If the terms match, the operation succeeds; otherwise, it results in a MatchError.

```
iex> a = 1
```

```
1
iex> 1 = a
1
iex> 2 = a
** (MatchError) no match of right hand side value: 1
```

In the above example, the first line binds the value 1 to the variable a. The second example succeeds because the value on the LHS (1) matches the value of a (which is also 1). However, the third line results in an error because 2 cannot match a, which holds the value 1.

Pattern Matching with Atoms

Atoms are constants where their name is their value. They are a fundamental data type in Elixir.

```
iex> my_atom = :elixir
:elixir
iex> :elixir = my_atom
:elixir
```

Here, my_atom is matched successfully to the atom :elixir. Therefore, the matching operation will pass, as both the LHS and RHS are the same.

Pattern Matching with Tuples

Tuples are fixed-size ordered collections of values and can be used seamlessly with pattern matching.

```
iex> {a, b, c} = {:ok, "hello", 42}
{:ok, "hello", 42}
iex> a
:ok
iex> b
"hello"
iex> c
42
```

In this example, the tuple on the RHS is deconstructed into the individual components on the LHS, binding a to :ok, b to "hello", and c to 42. If there were any mismatch in the structure, such as a tuple of a different size or different values, an error would occur.

Pattern Matching with Lists

Lists are collections of items. They can be of varying lengths and be nested. Pattern matching with lists usually involves the head (hd) and the tail (tl).

```
iex> [h | t] = [1, 2, 3, 4, 5]
[1, 2, 3, 4, 5]
iex> h
```

```
1
iex> t
[2, 3, 4, 5]
```

In this scenario, the list on the RHS is split into the head (h, which is 1) and the tail (t, which is [2, 3, 4, 5]). This kind of pattern matching is particularly useful in recursive functions operating on lists.

Pattern Matching with Maps

Maps are key-value stores in Elixir. When pattern matching with maps, only the specified keys need to be matched.

```
iex> %{"name" => name} = %{"name" => "Alice", "age" => 30}
%{"name" => "Alice", "age" => 30}
iex> name
"Alice"
```

In this context, only the "name" key needs to exist in the RHS map for the pattern match to succeed, allowing name to be bound to "Alice".

Each example given demonstrates the powerful, expressive nature of Elixir's pattern matching, making it integral in not only variable assignments but also within the broader scope of function definitions and control flow structures. Elixir's pattern matching can handle complex nesting and varied data types, ensuring robust and readable code.

3.3 Pattern Matching with Lists and Tuples

Pattern matching in Elixir extends beyond basic data types, playing a significant role when working with more complex data structures like lists and tuples. Understanding how to deconstruct and match these structures is essential for writing idiomatic and efficient Elixir code.

Pattern matching with lists allows us to deconstruct and access list elements directly. Lists in Elixir are implemented as linked lists, making pattern matching an effective way to handle operations on lists.

To match a list, we can use the cons operator |, which splits a list into its head and tail. For instance, consider the following pattern matching:

```
[head | tail] = [1, 2, 3]
```

In this example, head will be bound to 1, and tail will be bound to [2, 3]. This mechanism allows us to recursively process each element of the list.

We can match specific values and structures as well:

```
[1, 2 | [3, 4]] = [1, 2, 3, 4]
```

Here, the left side matches against the right side, yielding a successful pattern match. However, the following would not match:

```
[1, 2 | [3, 4]] = [1, 2, 'three', 4]
```

This is because the right side does not conform to the structure specified on the left side.

A more complex example involves nested lists:

```
[a, b, [c | d]] = [1, 2, [3, 4, 5]]
```

In this pattern, a will be 1, b will be 2, c will be 3, and d will be $[4, 5]$.

In function definitions, pattern matching with lists can be particularly powerful. Consider a function to calculate the length of a list:

```
defmodule ListUtils do
  def length([]), do: 0
  def length([_head | tail]), do: 1 + length(tail)
end
```

This function utilizes pattern matching to recursively count the elements of the list. The base case matches an empty list $[]$, returning 0, while the recursive case deconstructs the list, counting the head and calling itself with the tail.

Tuples can also be matched in a similar manner. Tuples are fixed-size collections of values, useful for grouping smaller pieces of data. Pattern matching with tuples allows for extracting individual elements succinctly:

```
{a, b, c} = {1, 2, 3}
```

After this operation, a will be 1, b will be 2, and c will be 3. Tuples must match the exact structure in terms of both size and position for the pattern match to be successful.

Pattern matching tuples is also frequently used in return values, especially in cases where functions return error tuples:

```
case File.read("path/to/file") do
  {:ok, content} -> IO.puts("File content: \#\{content\}")
  {:error, reason} -> IO.puts("Failed to read file: \#\{reason\}")
end
```

In this example, the File.read/1 function returns a tuple. The case expression uses pattern matching to differentiate between the :ok and :error atoms, handling each case accordingly.

We can combine lists and tuples for more advanced pattern matching. For example:

```
[{key1, value1}, {key2, value2}] = [{:name, "Alice"}, {:age, 30}]
```

Here, each element in the list is a tuple, allowing us to extract the keys and values from a list of tuples.

Patterns can also contain placeholders to ignore values. This is achieved using the underscore _, allowing us to focus only on the elements of interest:

```
[{_key1, value1}, {_key2, value2}] = [{:name, "Bob"}, {:age, 25}]
```

In scenarios where we need to work with nested structures, pattern matching remains straightforward and efficient:

```
list = [{:person, {:name, "Charlie", :age, 28}}, {:company, {:name, "Acme Corp"}}]
[{:person, {:name, person_name, :age, person_age}} | _] = list
```

Here, person_name will be "Charlie" and person_age will be 28.

Mastering pattern matching with lists and tuples is a crucial skill that enhances the ability to work with complex data in Elixir. It allows for expressive and efficient code, enabling developers to leverage Elixir's powerful pattern matching capabilities fully.

3.4 Using Pattern Matching in Function Definitions

Pattern matching in function definitions is one of the most powerful features of the Elixir programming language. By allowing multiple function clauses with different patterns, Elixir enables developers to write expressive and concise code. Each pattern acts as a filter, and the function clause whose pattern matches the given arguments is the one that gets executed. This section delves into the mechanics of using pattern matching in function definitions, covering various practical examples and best practices.

Consider a simple function that demonstrates basic pattern matching:

```
defmodule Example do
  def greet(:morning, name) do
    "Good morning, #{name}!"
  end

  def greet(:afternoon, name) do
    "Good afternoon, #{name}!"
  end

  def greet(:evening, name) do
    "Good evening, #{name}!"
  end
end
```

The greet/2 function above has three clauses, each matching a different atom (i.e., :morning, :afternoon, :evening) as its first argument, with name as the second argument. The appropriate clause is selected based on the value of the atom passed.

```
iex> Example.greet(:morning, "Alice")
"Good morning, Alice!"

iex> Example.greet(:afternoon, "Bob")
"Good afternoon, Bob!"
```

This demonstrates basic pattern matching, but Elixir's capabilities extend further. One of the more advanced uses involves matching nested data structures.

```
defmodule Rectangle do
  def area({width, height}) do
    width * height
  end
end
```

In the area/1 function, the pattern is a tuple consisting of two elements: width and height. When a tuple is passed to the area/1 function, its elements are destructured and bound to the variables within the function body.

```
iex> Rectangle.area({4, 5})
20

iex> Rectangle.area({6, 7})
42
```

Elixir's pattern matching also allows combining basic data types and more complex structures, such as lists or maps. For example, a function could compute the sum of the first two elements of a list:

```
defmodule Math do
  def sum_first_two([a, b | _]) do
    a + b
  end
end
```

The pattern [a, b | _] matches any list with at least two elements. The first two elements are bound to a and b, respectively, while the rest of the list is ignored.

```
iex> Math.sum_first_two([3, 4, 5, 6])
7

iex> Math.sum_first_two([10, 20])
30
```

Pattern matching in maps functions similarly:

```
defmodule User do
  def greet_user(%{name: name, age: age}) do
    "Hello, #{name}. You are #{age} years old."
  end
end
```

The pattern %name: name, age: age matches a map containing keys :name and :age. The values of these keys are bound to name and age.

```
iex> User.greet_user(%{name: "Alice", age: 30})
"Hello, Alice. You are 30 years old."

iex> User.greet_user(%{name: "Bob", age: 25})
"Hello, Bob. You are 25 years old."
```

Using guards in function definitions provides a way to extend pattern matching rules. Guards are additional constraints that must be satisfied for a pattern to match. They are specified using when keyword.

```
defmodule Number do
  def type(n) when is_integer(n) and n > 0 do
    "Positive integer"
  end

  def type(n) when is_integer(n) and n < 0 do
    "Negative integer"
  end

  def type(n) when is_integer(n) and n == 0 do
    "Zero"
  end
end
```

In this example, the type/1 function uses guards to dispatch based on the properties of the argument: positive, negative integer, or zero. Each clause has an accompanying guard that further refines the match.

```
iex> Number.type(42)
"Positive integer"

iex> Number.type(-7)
"Negative integer"

iex> Number.type(0)
"Zero"
```

In scenarios involving recursion, pattern matching can significantly simplify the logic. Take, for instance, reversing a list:

```
defmodule ListUtils do
  def reverse(list), do: reverse(list, [])

  defp reverse([], acc), do: acc

  defp reverse([head | tail], acc) do
    reverse(tail, [head | acc])
  end
end
```

Here, the public reverse/1 function delegates to a private helper reverse/2 which uses an accumulator acc. Through pattern matching, the function processes each element of the list recursively until the list is empty ([]), at which point the accumulator holds the reversed list.

```
iex> ListUtils.reverse([1, 2, 3])
[3, 2, 1]

iex> ListUtils.reverse([:a, :b, :c])
[:c, :b, :a]
```

These examples underscore the flexibility and potency of pattern matching in function definitions within Elixir. The ability to define multiple function clauses with distinct matching patterns facilitates clear, maintainable, and effective code.rained model. Continuing to

3.5 Control Structures: if, unless, and case

In Elixir, control structures provide the means to determine the flow of a program based on conditional evaluation. This section will delve into three fundamental control structures: if, unless, and case. Each of these constructs plays a significant role in directing the execution path of the code.

The if structure is used to execute a block of code if a specified condition evaluates to true. Its counterpart, unless, executes the block of code only if the condition evaluates to false. The case construct, on the other hand, allows matching against different patterns or values, executing the corresponding block for the first successful match.

if expressions follow the conventional if-else structure found in many other programming languages:

```
if condition do
  # code to execute if condition is true
else
```

```
  # code to execute if condition is false
end
```

The if keyword is followed by the condition to be evaluated. If the condition is true, the code within the do block will be executed. If the condition is false, the code within the else block will be executed. Consider the following example:

```
x = 10
if x > 5 do
  "x is greater than 5"
else
  "x is 5 or less"
end
```

In this case, since x is 10, the output will be:

```
"x is greater than 5"
```

unless is the inverse of if and is used to execute code only when a condition is false. Its structure mirrors that of the if construct:

```
unless condition do
  # code to execute if condition is false
else
  # code to execute if condition is true
end
```

For example:

```
x = 10
unless x > 15 do
  "x is 15 or less"
else
  "x is greater than 15"
end
```

Here, since x is 10, the output will be:

```
"x is 15 or less"
```

Moving on to the case construct, this provides a more powerful mechanism for conditional evaluation by allowing pattern matching against a value. Each case expression consists of a value to match against and multiple pattern clauses, structured as follows:

```
case value do
  pattern1 -> # code to execute if value matches pattern1
  pattern2 -> # code to execute if value matches pattern2
  _ -> # optional: code to execute if none of the patterns match
end
```

The case construct will attempt to match the value against each pattern in the sequence they are defined, executing the corresponding block for the first successful match. Here is an example:

```
case {3, 4, 5} do
  {1, x, 3} -> "Matched the pattern {1, x, 3}"
  {3, 4, 5} -> "Matched the pattern {3, 4, 5}"
  _ -> "No match found"
end
```

In this example, the value being matched is {3, 4, 5}. The case construct evaluates the patterns in order: - {1, x, 3} does not match. - {3, 4, 5} matches, so the resulting string is:

```
"Matched the pattern {3, 4, 5}"
```

If no pattern matches, an optional _ block can be provided to handle unmatched cases. The _ pattern is a wildcard that matches any value.

Using proper pattern matching with the case expression provides a clear and concise way to handle multiple conditions and values, which can significantly enhance the readability and maintainability of the code. By effectively leveraging if, unless, and case, Elixir programmers can write robust control structures that adapt to a wide range of scenarios.

3.6 The cond and with Statements

The cond and with statements in Elixir are powerful control structures that allow for more sophisticated branching and flow of control in program logic. Understanding these constructs is essential to writing efficient and readable Elixir code, particularly when dealing with complex conditions and transformations.

The cond Statement

The cond statement is used when you have multiple conditions to evaluate and you want to execute the block of code corresponding to the first condition that evaluates to true. It is akin to a series of if and else if constructs found in other programming languages, but provides a cleaner and more readable approach. Each condition is evaluated in sequence until a true condition is found. If no conditions match, an else block must be specified to handle any unmatched cases.

Here is the basic syntax of a cond statement:

```
cond do
  condition1 ->
    # Block of code if condition1 is true
  condition2 ->
```

```
    # Block of code if condition2 is true
  condition3 ->
    # Block of code if condition3 is true
  true ->
    # Block of code if none of the above conditions are true
end
```

An example will illustrate how cond can be used effectively in a real-world scenario. Suppose we want to categorize an integer into "negative", "zero", or "positive":

```
number = 5

result = cond do
  number < 0 ->
    "negative"
  number == 0 ->
    "zero"
  number > 0 ->
    "positive"
end

IO.puts(result)
```

```
positive
```

In this example, the cond statement checks the value of number and evaluates the corresponding condition. Since number is greater than zero, the string "positive" is returned and printed.

It is good practice to always include a 'true' condition as the last clause in a cond statement to handle unexpected cases. If no condition matches and no 'true' clause is provided, an error will be raised.

The with Statement

The with statement in Elixir is used to chain together a series of pattern matching operations, particularly in scenarios where you need to perform multiple matches that might fail. The with statement helps in keeping the code clean and reduces nesting, making the logic easier to follow.

The basic syntax of with is as follows:

```
with pattern1 <- expression1,
     pattern2 <- expression2,
     ...,
     do:
  # Block of code to execute if all patterns match
  ...
end
```

Each line in the with statement is a pattern match operation. If all patterns are matched successfully, the code block following do: is executed. If any match fails, the with expression immediately returns the value that failed to match.

Consider a practical example where we fetch user data from different sources and need to ensure all data points are valid:

```
fetch_user_data = fn ->
  with {:ok, user_id} <- get_user_id(),
       {:ok, user_info} <- get_user_info(user_id),
       {:ok, user_address} <- get_user_address(user_id) do
    {:ok, %{id: user_id, info: user_info, address: user_address}}
  else
    {:error, reason} -> {:error, reason}
  end
end
```

In this example, with is used to perform a sequence of operations related to fetching user data. If all operations are successful, the result is a map containing the user's ID, information, and address. If any operation fails, the corresponding error reason is returned.

This example demonstrates the power of with in handling multiple operations elegantly with minimal nesting. Each pattern match in the with statement corresponds to a step in the sequence, ensuring clean and readable code even for complex operations.

Both cond and with statements are essential tools in the Elixir programmer's toolkit. They provide clear advantages in terms of readability and efficiency when dealing with conditional logic and series of dependent operations respectively. Integrating these control structures effectively can significantly enhance your ability to write robust and maintainable Elixir code.

3.7 Error Handling with try, rescue, and catch

Error handling is an essential aspect of any robust software system. In Elixir, error handling can be elegantly managed using the constructs try, rescue, and catch. These constructs allow developers to handle exceptions gracefully, ensuring that the system remains stable even in the face of unexpected scenarios.

Elixir, being a modern functional language, provides a powerful error-handling strategy that aligns with its principles of immutability and pattern matching. This section delves into the syntactic structure and practical usage of try, rescue, and catch, elucidating their roles and demonstrating their applications through examples.

The try construct is foundational to exception handling in Elixir. It encapsulates a block of code that may potentially raise an exception. Here's a basic structure of a try block:

```
try do
  # Code that might raise an exception
rescue
  # Exception handling
end
```

Within the try block, you place the code that you suspect might fail. The rescue clause is then used to match and handle specific exceptions.

Consider the following example where an arithmetic operation could raise an exception due to division by zero:

```
def safe_divide(a, b) do
  try do
    a / b
  rescue
    ArithmeticError -> {:error, "Cannot divide by zero"}
  end
end
```

In this example, if b is zero, an ArithmeticError is raised. The rescue clause catches this exception and returns an appropriate error tuple.

Rescue clauses can pattern match on different types of exceptions. Suppose multiple types of exceptions need to be handled. You can extend the rescue block accordingly:

```
def handle_errors(value) do
  try do
    # Potentially risky operations
    String.to_atom(value)
  rescue
    ArgumentError -> {:error, "Invalid argument"}
    RuntimeError -> {:error, "Runtime error occurred"}
  end
end
```

In this case, both ArgumentError and RuntimeError are handled separately to provide specific error messages.

Next, let's discuss the catch construct, which is used to manage non-exception forms of errors, such as throwing a value. The catch block is slightly different and can capture thrown values:

```
try do
  throw(:error_occurred)
catch
```

```
  :throw, :error_occurred -> {:error, "A specific error was thrown"}
end
```

Here, the throw(:error_occurred) function explicitly throws a value, which is then caught by the catch clause. This is typically useful in control flow mechanisms where non-fatal error conditions need to be propagated.

An additional powerful feature in Elixir's error handling is the after clause, which ensures that certain code is run regardless of whether an exception was raised. This is analogous to the finally block in other programming languages. It is useful for cleanup operations:

```
def file_operation do
  try do
    {:ok, file} = File.open("sample.txt", [:read])
    # Perform file operations
  rescue
    File.Error -> {:error, "File operation failed"}
  after
    File.close(file)
  end
end
```

In this example, File.close(file) will be executed whether an exception was raised or not, ensuring that system resources are properly released.

The use of rescue, catch, and after within try blocks provides a comprehensive error-handling mechanism that helps manage exceptions and cleanup actions effectively.

Understanding and utilizing these constructs adeptly allows one to maintain control over the program flow, handle unexpected events gracefully, and ensure the stability and reliability of the system.

3.8 Using Guards in Function Clauses

In Elixir, guards offer a powerful mechanism to extend the capabilities of pattern matching in function clauses. Guards provide additional constraints that a match must satisfy, thereby allowing more specific and controlled execution paths in your function definitions.

Fundamentally, guards are Boolean expressions that can be used within function clauses to test certain conditions. They are introduced using the when keyword, following a pattern match. Here is the syntax outline for defining function clauses with guards:

```
def function_name(parameter) when guard_expression do
  # function body
end
```

To illustrate, consider defining a function that classifies a number as positive, negative, or zero. Using guards, the Elixir code can be made precise and readable:

```
defmodule NumberClassifier do

  def classify(number) when number > 0 do
    "positive"
  end

  def classify(number) when number < 0 do
    "negative"
  end

  def classify(0), do: "zero"

end
```

Here, the classify function has three distinct clauses. The first clause matches if the number is greater than zero, the second if the number is less than zero, and the third directly matches the literal zero. This pattern ensures that all integer inputs are processed correctly according to their sign.

Allowed Guard Expressions

Elixir restricts the set of expressions permitted in guards to ensure they remain efficient and free of side effects. Some of the commonly used allowed expressions include:

- Comparison operators: ==, !=, <, >, <=, >=
- Boolean operators: and, or, not
- Arithmetic operators: +, -, *, /
- Type checking functions: is_atom/1, is_binary/1, is_bitstring/1, is_boolean/1, is_float/1, is_function/1 & 2, is_integer/1, is_list/1, is_map/1, is_number/1, is_pid/1, is_port/1, is_reference/1, is_tuple/1
- Others: -, |>, ++, --, length/1, hd/1, tl/1

Combining Guards

Multiple guard clauses can be combined using both the 'and' and 'or' keywords. Consider the following example where we extend the number classification to categorize integers and floats separately:

```
defmodule ExtendedNumberClassifier do
  def classify(number) when is_integer(number) and number > 0 do
    "positive integer"
  end

  def classify(number) when is_float(number) and number > 0.0 do
    "positive float"
  end

  def classify(number) when is_integer(number) and number < 0 do
    "negative integer"
  end

  def classify(number) when is_float(number) and number < 0.0 do
    "negative float"
  end

  def classify(0), do: "zero"

  def classify(0.0), do: "zero"
end
```

Guard Sequences

In situations where multiple guards need to be applied in sequence, they can be separated by commas. A function clause can have multiple guard expressions that all must evaluate to true for the clause to match:

```
defmodule ValidateContent do
  def check_binary(data) when is_binary(data), do: :ok
  def check_binary(_), do: {:error, "Not a binary"}

  def check_length(data) when is_binary(data) and byte_size(data) > 4 do
    :ok
  end
  def check_length(_), do: {:error, "Insufficient length"}

end
```

In this example, the module ValidateContent has functions to check whether data is binary and whether it has a sufficient length. The second function clause, check_length, uses a guard to ensure both conditions are met.

Utilizing Guards in Real Applications

Guards are critical in real-world applications to validate function inputs and maintain robust and error-free code. For example, in a web application, input validation can be cleanly managed using guards:

```
defmodule UserRegistration do

  def register_user(%{age: age}) when is_integer(age) and age >= 18 do
    {:ok, "User registered"}
  end
  def register_user(%{age: _age}), do: {:error, "User must be 18 or older"}

  def register_user(_params), do: {:error, "Invalid parameters"}

end
```

This example demonstrates a user registration function where the registration is allowed only if the age is an integer and at least 18. Different clauses handle various invalid input scenarios.

Overall, guards enhance the precision and expressiveness of function clauses, enabling the function definitions to be more descriptive and safer. Proper utilization of guards ensures that all edge cases are adequately covered, making the resulting Elixir programs robust and maintainable.

Chapter 4

Functions and Modules

This chapter examines the creation and organization of functions and modules in Elixir. It covers defining functions, understanding function arity, and using multiple clauses. The chapter also addresses anonymous functions, higher-order functions, module definitions, and namespacing. Additionally, it includes importing and aliasing modules, defining module attributes and constants, and using docstrings and annotations for code documentation.

4.1 Defining Functions

In Elixir, functions are the foundational building blocks for creating reusable and modular code. Elixir supports two primary ways of defining functions: named functions within modules and anonymous functions. This section will focus on named functions.

Named functions are defined with the def keyword and are always encapsulated within a module. A module in Elixir is a collection of related functions and is defined using the defmodule keyword. The general structure for defining a module and a function is as follows:

```
defmodule ModuleName do
  def function_name(parameters) do
    # function body
  end
end
```

In the above template, ModuleName is the name of the module, function_name is the name of the function, and parameters are the arguments that the function accepts. The function body contains the sequence of expressions that define the function's behavior.

Consider the following example where a module named Math is defined with a single function add/2 that takes two parameters and returns their sum:

```
defmodule Math do
  def add(a, b) do
    a + b
  end
end
```

To invoke the add/2 function from the Math module, use the dot notation:

```
Math.add(1, 2)
```

This will output:

```
3
```

Functions in Elixir can be of any arity, which refers to the number of arguments a function takes. For instance, a function with two arguments has an arity of 2, and it is referred to as function_name/2. Elixir allows functions of the same name to be defined with different arities, supporting polymorphism through function overloading.

Here is an example to illustrate this concept:

```
defmodule Greeting do
  def say_hello() do
    "Hello, World!"
  end

  def say_hello(name) do
    "Hello, #{name}!"
  end
end
```

In this example, the Greeting module contains two functions with the same name say_hello, but with different arities. The first say_hello/0 takes no parameters and returns a generic greeting, whereas the second say_hello/1 takes one parameter name and returns a personalized greeting.

To invoke these functions:

```
Greeting.say_hello()
Greeting.say_hello("Alice")
```

The output will be:

```
"Hello, World!"
"Hello, Alice!"
```

Elixir functions also support multiple clauses, allowing for more expressive and concise definitions through pattern matching on function parameters. Multiple clauses are defined by providing multiple def blocks within the same function name. Consider the following example:

```
defmodule Factorial do
  def of(0), do: 1
  def of(n) when n > 0 do
    n * of(n - 1)
  end
end
```

In the Factorial module, the of/1 function is defined using two clauses. The first clause matches when the parameter is 0 and returns 1. The second clause matches when the parameter is a positive integer and calculates the factorial recursively. Notice the use of the guard clause, when n > 0, to ensure that the function only accepts positive integers.

Invoking the function:

```
Factorial.of(5)
```

The output will be:

```
120
```

Guards are a powerful feature in Elixir that allow you to add additional conditions to your pattern matching. Guards use the when keyword followed by a guard expression. Common expressions used in guards include comparisons (e.g., <, >, <=, >=), type checks (e.g., is_integer/1, is_float/1), and logical operators (e.g., and, or, not).

Consider the following example which uses guards for parameter validation:

```
defmodule NumberCheck do
  def is_even(n) when is_integer(n) and rem(n, 2) == 0, do: true
  def is_even(_), do: false
end
```

Here, the is_even/1 function checks if a given integer is even. The first clause uses a guard to ensure the parameter is an integer and that the remainder when divided by 2 is 0. If these conditions are met, the function returns true; otherwise, it falls back to the second clause, returning false.

To check if a number is even:

```
NumberCheck.is_even(4)
NumberCheck.is_even(3)
```

The output will be:

```
true
false
```

Functions in Elixir are equipped with the ability to explicitly state their intended functionality through comments and documentation. Adding a block of comments directly above the function definition provides inline documentation, aiding in readability and maintainability.

Elixir's built-in tool ExDoc leverages these inline comments to generate extensive documentation. Use the @doc attribute for block comments:

```
defmodule DocumentedMath do
  @doc """
  Adds two numbers.

  ## Examples

      iex> DocumentedMath.add(1, 2)
      3

  """
  def add(a, b) do
    a + b
  end
end
```

This approach ensures that when the DocumentedMath module is examined, the ExDoc generated documentation will include the function description and sample usage, thereby making the function's purpose and usage clear.

Thus, defining functions in Elixir encompasses more than mere syntax. Understanding arity, multiple clauses, guards, and documenting functions are all pivotal in crafting robust, maintainable, and self-explanatory code.

4.2 Function Arity and Multiple Clauses

In Elixir, the concept of arity is fundamental. Arity refers to the number of arguments a function takes. Each function is uniquely identified by its name and arity, not just by its name. This distinction facilitates the creation of multiple functions with the same name but different arities in the same module.

Consider the following examples in the lstlisting environment:

```
defmodule Math do
  def add(a, b) do
    a + b
  end

  def add(a, b, c) do
    a + b + c
  end
end
```

Here, Math.add/2 is a different function from Math.add/3. The /2 and /3 suffixes denote the arity of each function.

Elixir supports defining functions with multiple clauses, allowing for more expressive and pattern-matched function definitions. Multiple clauses provide mechanisms to handle different patterns of inputs elegantly. When defining functions with multiple clauses, Elixir evaluates each clause in the order it is defined. The first clause that matches the given arguments is executed.

Consider the following example:

```
defmodule Factorial do
  def calc(0), do: 1
  def calc(n) when n > 0 do
    n * calc(n - 1)
  end
end
```

In this Factorial module, the calc/1 function has two clauses. The first clause matches when the argument is 0, and it returns 1. The second clause matches when the argument is any positive integer, leveraging the when guard clause. If the argument is greater than 0, the function recursively calculates the factorial.

```
iex> Factorial.calc(0)
1
iex> Factorial.calc(5)
120
```

Pattern matching is essential in multiple clause definitions. Each clause can match different shapes or types of input. Here is an example of a function that processes a list in different ways based on its contents:

```
defmodule ListProcessor do
  def process([]), do: "Empty list"
  def process([head | tail]) do
    "Head: #{head}, Tail: #{inspect(tail)}"
  end
end
```

When this function is called, it handles empty lists and non-empty lists differently.

```
iex> ListProcessor.process([])
"Empty list"
iex> ListProcessor.process([1, 2, 3])
"Head: 1, Tail: [2, 3]"
```

Multiple clauses can also be leveraged with function guards to refine the patterns being matched. Here are more detailed examples that use guards:

```
defmodule NumberAnalyzer do
  def analyze(n) when n < 0 do
    "Negative number"
  end
  def analyze(0), do: "Zero"
  def analyze(n) when n > 0 and rem(n, 2) == 0 do
    "Positive even number"
  end
  def analyze(n) when n > 0 and rem(n, 2) != 0 do
    "Positive odd number"
  end
end
```

These clauses handle various cases: negative numbers, zero, positive even numbers, and positive odd numbers.

```
iex> NumberAnalyzer.analyze(-1)
"Negative number"
iex> NumberAnalyzer.analyze(0)
"Zero"
iex> NumberAnalyzer.analyze(4)
"Positive even number"
iex> NumberAnalyzer.analyze(7)
"Positive odd number"
```

Functions with different arities can co-exist within a module by defining multiple clauses for each arity. When invoking these functions, Elixir will select the one with the matching arity and pattern-match the arguments to determine the correct clause to execute.

Through the application of function arity and multiple clauses, Elixir code becomes more robust, readable, and efficient. This structure allows precise function definitions and seamless handling of complex input patterns, ensuring code clarity and correctness.

4.3 Anonymous Functions and the fn Keyword

Anonymous functions in Elixir are defined using the fn keyword. Unlike named functions which are defined within a module and associated with a name, anonymous functions do not have a name and are often used as expressions. They are useful in scenarios where functions are utilized briefly and passed as arguments without necessitating a named definition.

To declare an anonymous function, the fn keyword is followed by the parameter list and the function body. Each clause in the function is separated by the -> symbol, and multiple clauses are handled akin to named functions by commensurately using conditional logic.

Consider the following example:

```
add = fn (a, b) -> a + b end
```

In this instance, add is an anonymous function that takes two arguments, a and b, and returns their sum. The function body, encapsulated between fn and end, consists of a single expression.

Executing the above function should yield the following results:

```
iex> add.(5, 3)
8
```

Notice the use of the dot notation, add.(5, 3), to invoke the anonymous function. This syntax is requisite for anonymous functions in Elixir.

Anonymous functions can also include more complicated logic spanning multiple clauses:

```
compare = fn
  (a, b) when a > b -> :greater
  (a, b) when a < b -> :lesser
  (a, b) -> :equal
end
```

Here, the compare function evaluates two parameters and returns one of three atoms: :greater, :lesser, or :equal, based on their values.

Evaluation for above function will result in:

```
iex> compare.(5, 3)
:greater

iex> compare.(2, 4)
:lesser

iex> compare.(7, 7)
:equal
```

This example highlights how guard clauses can be incorporated into anonymous functions, similar to named functions.

When defining anonymous functions inside other expressions or modules, the syntax remains consistent. Anonymous functions can be passed directly as arguments to higher-order functions, enriching their usage within passing functions dynamically:

```
list = [1, 2, 3, 4, 5]
Enum.map(list, fn x -> x * 2 end)
```

In this illustration, the anonymous function `fn x -> x * 2 end` is applied to each element of the `list` by the `Enum.map/2` function, resulting in a new list where each element is doubled:

```
iex> Enum.map(list, fn x -> x * 2 end)
[2, 4, 6, 8, 10]
```

Anonymous functions can be defined in a concise format using the `&` shorthand syntax. This shorthand allows for compact declarations, often improving readability for trivial functions:

```
multiply = &(&1 * &2)
```

In the example above, `&1` and `&2` denote the first and second arguments of the anonymous function respectively. The `multiply` function behaves the same as if it were defined using the `fn` syntax.

Execution of shorthand function results in:

```
iex> multiply.(4, 5)
20
```

To summarize, anonymous functions in Elixir, declared with the `fn` keyword, offer a flexible and succinct way of leveraging functions without assigning names. They integrate seamlessly with higher-order functions and allow for complex logic through multiple clauses and guards. The `&` shorthand syntax further enhances their succinctness, facilitating more readable and maintainable code in scenarios where brevity is favored.

4.4 Higher-Order Functions

Higher-order functions are a distinctive feature of functional programming languages, including Elixir, providing significant expressive power and flexibility. A higher-order function is a function that can take one or more functions as arguments and/or return a function as its result. This allows for functional composition, abstraction over behavior, and concise expression of complex logic.

In Elixir, higher-order functions can be defined and used seamlessly, thanks to the language's first-class treatment of functions. To understand higher-order functions comprehensively, we will explore several core aspects: passing functions as arguments, returning functions, and the practical use cases of higher-order functions in Elixir programming.

To illustrate how higher-order functions work, consider the following example, where a function is passed as an argument to another function:

```
defmodule HigherOrderExample do
  def apply_function(func, value) do
    func.(value)
  end
end

increment = fn x -> x + 1 end
result = HigherOrderExample.apply_function(increment, 5)
IO.puts(result) # Outputs: 6
```

The apply_function/2 function takes a function, func, and a value, value. It applies the function to the value using the dot-parentheses syntax (func.(value)). In this case, the anonymous function increment adds 1 to its argument, and when passed to apply_function/2 with the value 5, the result is 6.

Higher-order functions can also return functions. This can be particularly useful for creating function factories or decorators. Here is an example of a higher-order function returning another function:

```
defmodule HigherOrderExample do
  def make_adder(n) do
    fn x -> x + n end
  end
end

add_five = HigherOrderExample.make_adder(5)
result = add_five.(10)
IO.puts(result) # Outputs: 15
```

In the above code, make_adder/1 is a higher-order function that takes a number n and returns an anonymous function. This anonymous function takes another number x and adds it to n. The returned function can then be used as add_five, which adds 5 to any given number.

Another common use of higher-order functions in Elixir is with the Enum module, which provides a collection of functions for enumerables. Many of these functions take other functions as arguments to perform operations on lists, maps, and other collections. For example:

```
list = [1, 2, 3, 4, 5]
squared_list = Enum.map(list, fn x -> x * x end)
IO.inspect(squared_list) # Outputs: [1, 4, 9, 16, 25]
```

In this example, Enum.map/2 is a higher-order function that takes a list and a function. It applies the function to each element of the list and returns a new list with the results. The anonymous function fn x -> x * x end computes the square of each element.

Higher-order functions also facilitate the creation of more abstract, reusable code components. For instance, consider a function that filters elements from a list based on a given criterion:

```
defmodule HigherOrderExample do
  def filter(list, func) do
    Enum.filter(list, func)
  end
end

is_even = fn x -> rem(x, 2) == 0 end
even_numbers = HigherOrderExample.filter([1, 2, 3, 4, 5], is_even)
IO.inspect(even_numbers) # Outputs: [2, 4]
```

Here, filter/2 is defined in the HigherOrderExample module and uses Enum.filter/2 internally, showcasing the power of combining higher-order functions. The anonymous function is_even checks if a number is even, and it is passed to filter/2 to extract the even numbers from the list.

Through these examples, it becomes evident that higher-order functions enrich Elixir's functional programming paradigm by allowing greater modularity, abstraction, and composability in code.

4.5 Modules and Namespaces

Modules are a foundational construct in Elixir, providing a way to encapsulate and organize functions, types, and other resources. They enable better code organization and reuse, promoting modularity and maintainability in Elixir projects. A module in Elixir is defined using the defmodule keyword.

```
defmodule MathOperations do
  def add(a, b) do
    a + b
  end

  def subtract(a, b) do
    a - b
  end

  def multiply(a, b) do
    a * b
  end

  def divide(a, b) do
    a / b
  end
end
```

In the above example, MathOperations is a module that encapsulates basic arithmetic operations. Each function within the module can be called using the dot notation, prefixed by the module name, like so:

```
MathOperations.add(5, 3)
MathOperations.subtract(10, 4)
```

8
6

Modules in Elixir also allow nested modules, providing a way to namespace related functionalities. Nesting modules help in preventing naming conflicts and organizing code into logical groups.

```
defmodule Geometry do
  defmodule Rectangle do
    def area(length, width) do
      length * width
    end

    def perimeter(length, width) do
      2 * (length + width)
    end
  end

  defmodule Circle do
    def area(radius) do
      :math.pi() * radius * radius
    end

    def circumference(radius) do
      2 * :math.pi() * radius
    end
  end
end
```

To call functions in nested modules, use the full module path as shown below:

```
Geometry.Rectangle.area(5, 3)
Geometry.Circle.circumference(4)
```

```
15
25.132741228718345
```

Elixir also provides mechanisms for importing functionalities from other modules into the current module. This can be done using the import keyword. Importing allows direct access to functions without needing to reference the module name.

```
defmodule Main do
  import MathOperations

  def perform_operations do
    IO.puts add(10, 5)
    IO.puts multiply(6, 7)
  end
end

Main.perform_operations()
```

```
15
42
```

The alias keyword can be used to create module name aliases. This is particularly helpful when dealing with long module names or deeply nested modules.

```
defmodule Main do
  alias Geometry.Circle

  def display_area(radius) do
    IO.puts Circle.area(radius)
  end
end

Main.display_area(7)
```

```
153.93804002589985
```

Another powerful feature of Elixir is use, which is a macro that allows a module to leverage the functionality of another module. Often used in conjunction with behaviours, use can inject code into the current module.

```
defmodule Greeter do
  defmacro __using__(_) do
    quote do
      def greet(name) do
        IO.puts "Hello, #{name}!"
      end
    end
  end
```

```
end

defmodule Main do
  use Greeter
end

Main.greet("Alice")
```

```
Hello, Alice!
```

Modules in Elixir thus provide robust capabilities for organizing, encapsulating, and managing code. The use of nested modules, import, alias, and use enhances code readability and reusability, promoting efficient development practices.

4.6 Importing and Aliasing Modules

In Elixir, the ability to manage and organize code efficiently through modules is a fundamental feature. To facilitate reusability and maintainability, it is essential to understand how to import and alias modules. These functionalities allow developers to access functions and macros from other modules, avoid name collisions, and shorten module names for convenience.

Modules are typically defined in separate files. To use functions from these modules without qualifying them every time, Elixir provides two main mechanisms: import and alias.

Importing Modules

The import directive allows functions and macros from another module to be used directly without needing to prefix them with the module name. This can significantly reduce verbosity in the code.

For example, consider a module MathUtils defined as follows:

```
defmodule MathUtils do
  def add(a, b) do
    a + b
  end

  def subtract(a, b) do
    a - b
  end
end
```

To use the functions add and subtract without prefixing them with MathUtils, you can use the import directive:

```
defmodule Calculator do
  import MathUtils

  def calculate do
    add(5, 3) # directly using the add function
    subtract(5, 3) # directly using the subtract function
  end
end
```

When using import, you can also specify function names and their arity to limit what gets imported:

```
defmodule Calculator do
  import MathUtils, only: [add: 2]

  def calculate do
    add(5, 3) # directly using the add function
  end
end
```

In this example, only the add/2 function from MathUtils is imported.

Aliasing Modules

The alias directive is used to shorten module names, which can help with readability and reduce typing effort. It is particularly useful when working with deeply nested module names.

Consider a module MyApp.Utilities.Math defined as:

```
defmodule MyApp.Utilities.Math do
  def multiply(a, b) do
    a * b
  end

  def divide(a, b) do
    a / b
  end
end
```

Referring to MyApp.Utilities.Math every time you want to use its functions can be cumbersome. The alias directive can be used to give it a shorter alias:

```
defmodule Calculator do
  alias MyApp.Utilities.Math

  def calculate do
    Math.multiply(5, 3) # using the shortened alias Math
    Math.divide(10, 2) # using the shortened alias Math
  end
end
```

You can also provide a custom alias name:

```
defmodule Calculator do
```

```
  alias MyApp.Utilities.Math, as: MathUtils

  def calculate do
    MathUtils.multiply(5, 3) # using the custom alias MathUtils
    MathUtils.divide(10, 2) # using the custom alias MathUtils
  end
end
```

Utilizing import and alias together can help manage large codebases more efficiently. However, it is important to use these directives judiciously to maintain code clarity and prevent namespace pollution. Properly importing only necessary functions and using clear alias names will ensure code remains readable and maintainable.

To demonstrate the execution of the Calculator.calculate function which uses imported and aliased modules, consider the following Elixir script in the calculator.exs file:

```
defmodule MathUtils do
  def add(a, b) do
    a + b
  end

  def subtract(a, b) do
    a - b
  end
end

defmodule MyApp.Utilities.Math do
  def multiply(a, b) do
    a * b
  end

  def divide(a, b) do
    a / b
  end
end

defmodule Calculator do
  import MathUtils, only: [add: 2, subtract: 2]
  alias MyApp.Utilities.Math

  def calculate do
    add_result = add(5, 3)
    subtract_result = subtract(5, 3)
    multiply_result = Math.multiply(5, 3)
    divide_result = Math.divide(10, 2)

    {add_result, subtract_result, multiply_result, divide_result}
  end
end

IO.inspect(Calculator.calculate)
```

Executing the script will produce the following output:

```
{8, 2, 15, 5.0}
```

This output confirms that the functions from both MathUtils and MyApp.Utilities.Math were properly imported and aliased, allowing for seamless integration and usage within the Calculator module.

4.7 Attribute Definitions and Module Constants

Elixir allows for the definition of module attributes, which can serve as constants or metadata about the module. Understanding how to define and use these attributes effectively is essential for writing clean and maintainable Elixir code.

Module attributes are defined using the @ symbol followed by their name. These attributes can then be assigned values that remain constant for the lifecycle of the module. One of the primary uses for module attributes is to create constants that can be reused throughout the module, enhancing code readability and maintainability.

Here is an example of defining a module attribute as a constant:

```
defmodule MathConstants do
  @pi 3.14159
  @e 2.71828

  def pi, do: @pi
  def e, do: @e
end
```

In this example, @pi and @e are defined as module attributes representing the mathematical constants π and e, respectively. These attributes are then accessed within the module through the pi/0 and e/0 functions. By defining them as module attributes, any changes to their values would only need to be made in one place, simplifying maintenance.

Module attributes can also serve as metadata. For instance, Elixir makes use of several predefined attributes for documentation and code organization, such as @doc, @moduledoc, and @behaviour. Here's how you might use these attributes:

```
defmodule Example do
  @moduledoc """
  This module provides example functions to illustrate
  how to use module attributes in Elixir.
  """

  @doc "Calculates the square of a number."
  def square(x), do: x * x
```

```
  @doc since: "1.0.0", deprecated: "Use new_function/1 instead."
  def old_function(x), do: x * x
end
```

In this code, @moduledoc provides module-level documentation, while @doc provides function-level documentation. The latter can also include metadata such as the version since which the function is available and deprecation information, which is helpful in larger projects where functions may evolve over time.

Elixir's build tool, Mix, along with the ExDoc library, uses these documentation attributes to generate HTML documentation for projects, making it convenient for developers to understand the purpose and usage of various modules and functions.

Elixir also allows for the use of computed module attributes. These attributes can be assigned values based on other values, enabling conditional logic at compile time. For instance:

```
defmodule CompileTimeConfig do
  @env Mix.env()
  @moduledoc """
  Module behavior is configured based on the environment.
  Current environment: #{@env}
  """

  @doc "Returns true if current environment is :dev."
  def dev_env?(), do: @env == :dev
end
```

Here, the @env attribute is computed at compile time using Mix.env/0, which retrieves the current environment. This allows CompileTimeConfig to behave differently based on whether it is running in development, test, or production environments. Documentation can even include dynamic content by embedding the value of @env within the @moduledoc attribute.

It's crucial to note that module attributes are immutable once defined, meaning their value cannot change over the lifetime of the module. Attempting to reassign an attribute will result in a compile-time error. This characteristic ensures that constants and meta-information remain consistent and reliable throughout the module's execution.

When defining constants, it's also possible to use pattern matching with module attributes, as demonstrated below:

```
defmodule StatusCodes do
  @status_ok 200
  @status_not_found 404

  def status_message(@status_ok), do: "OK"
```

```
  def status_message(@status_not_found), do: "Not Found"
end
```

In this module, the attributes @status_ok and @status_not_found represent HTTP status codes. The status_message/1 function uses pattern matching to return corresponding status messages.

Module attributes are a powerful feature in Elixir, enabling the definition of constants, configuration based on compile-time values, and the addition of metadata for documentation purposes. Their immutability and integration with the Mix toolchain make them a reliable and essential part of Elixir programming.

4.8 Docstrings and Annotations

Docstrings and annotations serve as essential tools for documenting code in Elixir. They enhance the readability and maintainability of your code by providing necessary context and explanations. Docstrings are used for documenting modules, functions, and macros, while annotations can add metadata to functions and variables. The combination of these practices ensures the codebase remains accessible and understandable, both for the original author and for others who may work with the code in the future.

In Elixir, docstrings can be added using the @doc attribute. This attribute supports both module-level and function-level documentation. Below is a step-by-step guide to using docstrings in Elixir.

Adding a docstring to a module involves placing the @moduledoc attribute at the beginning of the module. This attribute accepts a string that describes the module's purpose and functionality.

```
defmodule Math do
  @moduledoc """
  Provides basic mathematical functions such as addition,
  subtraction, multiplication, and division.
  """
end
```

Function-level documentation is achieved using the @doc attribute, which should be placed immediately before the function definition. This attribute also accepts a string that describes the function's behavior, input parameters, and output.

```
defmodule Math do
  @moduledoc """
```

```
  Provides basic mathematical functions such as addition,
  subtraction, multiplication, and division.
  """

  @doc """
  Adds two numbers.

  ## Parameters
  - x: The first number.
  - y: The second number.

  ## Examples
      iex> Math.add(2, 3)
      5

  """
  def add(x, y) do
    x + y
  end
end
```

In the example above, the @doc attribute is used to append documentation to the add/2 function. The docstring includes a brief description of the function, a section for parameters, and an example usage that can be tested in the Elixir Interactive Shell (IEx).

Annotations provide metadata about the code elements. Common annotations in Elixir include @spec for specifying types and @type for defining custom types. The @spec annotation helps in defining the type specifications of a function, which can be useful for static analysis and type checking.

```
defmodule Math do
  @moduledoc """
  Provides basic mathematical functions such as addition,
  subtraction, multiplication, and division.
  """

  @doc """
  Adds two numbers.

  ## Parameters
  - x: The first number.
  - y: The second number.

  ## Examples
      iex> Math.add(2, 3)
      5

  """
  @spec add(number(), number()) :: number()
  def add(x, y) do
    x + y
  end
end
```

In this code, the @spec annotation specifies that both parameters x and y must be of type number(), and the function returns a number(). This usage helps in verifying that the function adheres to its specification.

Elixir also enables the definition of custom types using the @type attribute, allowing for more expressive and self-documenting code.

```
defmodule Shape do
  @moduledoc """
  Provides functionalities to handle geometric shapes.
  """

  @type point :: {number(), number()}

  @doc """
  Calculates the distance between two points.

  ## Parameters
  - p1: The first point as a tuple \(x, y\).
  - p2: The second point as a tuple \(x, y\).

  """
  @spec distance(point(), point()) :: float()
  def distance({x1, y1}, {x2, y2}) do
    :math.sqrt(:math.pow(x2 - x1, 2) + :math.pow(y2 - y1, 2))
  end
end
```

In this example, the @type attribute defines a custom type point as a tuple consisting of two numbers. The @spec annotation is then used to specify the distance/2 function, demonstrating how custom types can provide clearer and more concise type annotations.

Using docstrings and annotations consistently ensures that the code is well-documented and conforms to expected usage patterns. This practice is beneficial not only for code readability but also for leveraging automated tools that rely on annotations for tasks like static analysis, thereby improving overall code quality and robustness.

Chapter 5

Concurrency with Processes

This chapter introduces concurrency in Elixir, detailing the actor model and the use of processes. It explains how to spawn processes, send and receive messages, and manage process lifecycles and exit signals. The chapter also covers process monitoring and linking, leveraging the Task module for simpler concurrency, and handling state with Agents. Practical examples illustrate building a simple application using these concepts.

5.1 Introduction to Concurrency in Elixir

Concurrency is a fundamental aspect of modern programming, allowing multiple tasks to be executed simultaneously. Elixir, a functional programming language designed for building scalable and maintainable applications, leverages the robust and well-established Erlang Virtual Machine (BEAM) to handle concurrency. This section presents the essential concepts of concurrency in Elixir, focusing on its implementation and benefits.

Elixir's concurrency model is based on the Actor Model. In this model, actors are the fundamental units of computation. Each actor is an independent entity that communicates with other actors through message passing, ensuring that no two actors share state. This design promotes fault tolerance and scalability, making it possible to build highly concurrent systems.

In Elixir, actors are implemented as processes. Processes in Elixir are not the same as operating system processes; they are lightweight, managed by the BEAM, and can be created in large numbers without significant overhead. Each process has its own state and executes independently. The lightweight nature allows Elixir applications to manage tens of thousands of concurrent processes efficiently.

To illustrate the creation and management of processes, consider the following example utilizing the spawn/1 function to create a new process.

```
defmodule ConcurrencyExample do
  def say_hello do
    IO.puts("Hello from a new process!")
  end
end

# Spawning a new process
pid = spawn(ConcurrencyExample, :say_hello, [])
```

In this example, the spawn/1 function takes the module name, function name, and an argument list to create a new process executing the say_hello/0 function. The spawn/1 function returns a process identifier (PID), which uniquely identifies the newly created process.

Processes communicate by sending and receiving messages. Elixir provides the send/2 function for sending messages to a process and the receive construct for handling incoming messages. Here's an example demonstrating this message passing mechanism:

```
defmodule Messenger do
  def receive_message do
    receive do
      {:hello, sender} ->
        IO.puts("Received hello from #{inspect sender}")
        send(sender, :hello_ack)
    end
  end
end

# Spawning a process that waits for a message
pid = spawn(Messenger, :receive_message, [])

# Sending a message to the spawned process
send(pid, {:hello, self()})

# Waiting for acknowledgment
receive do
  :hello_ack -> IO.puts("Acknowledgment received!")
end
```

In this code, a process is spawned to execute the receive_message/0 function. The main process sends a message to the spawned process, which then receives the message, processes it, and sends an acknowledgment back. The main process waits for and prints the acknowledgment.

The implementation of concurrency in Elixir presents several advantages:

- **Isolation:** Since processes do not share state, they are isolated from each other. This isolation minimizes side effects and simplifies debugging.
- **Lightweight:** Processes in Elixir are lightweight, allowing the creation of a large number of processes without significant overhead.
- **Fault Tolerance:** Process isolation leads to fault-tolerant systems. If a process crashes, it does not affect others, enabling the design of robust applications.
- **Scalability:** The ability to manage thousands of concurrent processes efficiently makes Elixir ideal for building scalable systems.

As we continue, we will explore more advanced topics such as the actor model and process lifecycle, and delve deeper into functions and constructs provided by Elixir to manage processes. Understanding these concepts will enable you to leverage the full power of concurrency in your applications.

5.2 The Actor Model and Processes

The Actor Model is a conceptual framework that treats "actors" as the fundamental units of computation. In this model, actors encapsulate state and behavior, interact solely through message passing, and do not share memory. This abstraction facilitates concurrent computation by allowing actors to execute independently and communicate asynchronously. Elixir, built on the Erlang VM (BEAM), embraces the Actor Model to handle concurrency effectively.

Processes in Elixir are lightweight and designed for large-scale concurrent applications. They serve as the realization of actors in Elixir, with each process being an independent thread of execution. Processes in

Elixir are isolated; they do not share state and communicate exclusively through messages. The Erlang runtime system can handle millions of processes concurrently due to their lightweight nature.

Creating processes in Elixir is straightforward. The spawn function is used to create a new process. For example, consider a simple case where a process prints a message:

```
defmodule Example do
  def say_hello do
    IO.puts("Hello, world!")
  end
end

spawn(Example, :say_hello, [])
```

The spawn function takes three arguments: the module name, the function name as an atom, and a list of arguments to pass to the function. Here, it creates a new process that invokes the Example.say_hello/0 function.

Processes can also be created using anonymous functions:

```
pid = spawn(fn -> IO.puts("Anonymous Hello") end)
```

In this example, an anonymous function containing IO.puts("Anonymous Hello") is spawned as a new process.

Inter-process communication is achieved through message passing using the send and receive constructs. Every process has a mailbox, where messages sent to it are stored. Messages are sent using the send function and received using the receive block.

The send function is used as follows:

```
send(pid, "Hello from another process")
```

Here, send/2 takes the process identifier pid and the message to send. The receive block waits for messages in the process's mailbox and pattern matches on them:

```
defmodule Receiver do
  def listen do
    receive do
      msg -> IO.puts("Received message: #{msg}")
    end
  end
end

pid = spawn(Receiver, :listen, [])
send(pid, "Hello")
```

In this implementation, the Receiver.listen/0 function waits for a message and prints it when received.

Processes in Elixir are not limited to sequential execution; they can also carry out loops or recurring tasks by recursively invoking themselves. For instance, a process can be made to continuously listen for and print messages:

```
defmodule LoopReceiver do
  def listen do
    receive do
      msg ->
        IO.puts("Received message: #{msg}")
        listen()
    end
  end
end

pid = spawn(LoopReceiver, :listen, [])
send(pid, "Hello, again")
send(pid, "Hello, world")
```

In the above code, after printing the received message, the LoopReceiver.listen/0 function recursively calls itself, thereby re-entering the receive block.

Processes can terminate in several ways. A process can naturally complete its work and terminate, or it can be explicitly terminated using the exit/2 function. The following example demonstrates a process that terminates itself after sending a message:

```
defmodule SelfTerminating do
  def run do
    send(self(), :done)
    exit(:normal)
  end
end

pid = spawn(SelfTerminating, :run, [])
```

The exit(:normal) call terminates the process with a reason of :normal, indicating a clean shutdown.

Processes can also supervise and monitor other processes, ensuring robust fault-tolerance. In the next sections, we delve deeper into managing process lifecycles, using process monitors, and leveraging supervision trees.

Understanding processes and the actor model is crucial for building concurrent systems in Elixir. Mastery of these concepts enables the development of resilient and scalable applications that exploit the advantages of concurrent computation provided by the BEAM.

5.3 Spawning Processes with spawn and spawn_link

In Elixir, the core functions for creating concurrent processes are spawn/1,2 and spawn_link/1,2. These functions allow developers to create new processes, each with an isolated state, which can execute functions independently.

spawn/1,2 allows for the creation of processes without linking them to the parent process. The spawn function returns the Process Identifier (PID) of the spawned process. This identifier can be used for message passing, process monitoring, and various other tasks. The following example demonstrates basic usage of spawn:

```
defmodule ProcessExample do
  def say_hello do
    IO.puts "Hello from a spawned process!"
  end
end
pid = spawn(ProcessExample, :say_hello, [])
```

In this example, the say_hello/0 function in the ProcessExample module is executed in a separate process. The spawn/3 function is used, where the first argument is the module name, the second argument is the function name (as an atom), and the third argument is a list of arguments to be passed to the function. The generated output would be:

```
Hello from a spawned process!
```

By creating processes with spawn, developers can effectively manage their code to handle concurrent operations. This is particularly useful in scenarios where tasks can run independently without affecting the flow of the main program.

spawn_link/1,2 works similarly to spawn/1,2 but creates a bi-directional link between the parent process and the spawned process. This means that if either process terminates (normally or abnormally), the linked process will also terminate. Linking processes is useful for creating greater fault-tolerance in a system-level manner. Here is how one would use spawn_link:

```
defmodule CrashExample do
  def crash do
    exit(:crashed)
  end
end
```

```
pid = spawn_link(CrashExample, :crash, [])
```

In this example, the crash/0 function causes the process to terminate by calling exit/1 with the reason :crashed. Since the processes are linked via spawn_link/3, the parent process will also terminate. This mechanism can be leveraged to monitor and restart processes as necessary, especially in applications where fault tolerance is critical.

To safely manage linked processes, Elixir provides mechanisms to handle process exits gracefully. One of these mechanisms is trapping exits. When a process traps exits, it does not terminate when a linked process terminates; instead, it receives a message in the format {:EXIT, pid, reason}. The following example demonstrates trapping exits:

```
defmodule ManageProcess do
  def start do
    Process.flag(:trap_exit, true)
    spawn_link(fn -> exit(:normal) end)
    receive do
      {:EXIT, _pid, reason} ->
        IO.puts "Linked process exited with reason: #{reason}"
    end
  end
end

ManageProcess.start()
```

In this example: 1. We set the process flag :trap_exit to true using Process.flag/2. 2. A linked process is created that will exit with the reason :normal. 3. The parent process then waits to receive the exit signal in the format {:EXIT, pid, reason}.

This setup helps in creating sophisticated supervision trees, where supervisors can monitor the health of worker processes and restart them when they terminate unexpectedly.

It is essential to differentiate between synchronous and asynchronous workflows when working with spawn and spawn_link. Since spawn/3 and spawn_link/3 execute the function body asynchronously, the parent process continues execution without waiting for the child process to complete.

Building on this knowledge, the next section will examine message passing between processes, enabling inter-process communication to coordinate the tasks executed concurrently.

5.4 Sending and Receiving Messages

In Elixir, processes communicate with each other by sending and receiving messages, a fundamental aspect of the actor model. Every process has a mailbox that stores messages until they are processed. The capabilities of sending and receiving messages enable the development of highly concurrent applications.

Elixir provides the send/2 function to send messages and the receive/1 block to receive them. The send/2 function takes two arguments: the PID (process identifier) of the receiving process and the message itself. The receive/1 block is used to handle incoming messages in the context of a process.

To demonstrate the process of sending and receiving messages, we begin by spawning a new process that can handle messages. The following code snippet showcases this concept:

```
defmodule MessageHandler do
  def start do
    spawn(fn -> loop() end)
  end

  defp loop do
    receive do
      {sender, message} ->
        IO.puts("Received message: #{message}")
        send(sender, {:ok, "Message received"})
        loop()
    end
  end
end
```

In this module, the start/0 function spawns a new process that runs the loop/0 function. The loop/0 function enters a receive/1 block, waiting for incoming messages. When a message is received, it pattern matches on a tuple containing the sender's PID and the message. It then prints the message to the console and sends an acknowledgment back to the sender.

The sending process can interact with the MessageHandler module as follows:

```
pid = MessageHandler.start()
send(pid, {self(), "Hello, process!"})

receive do
  {:ok, response} -> IO.puts("Got response: #{response}")
  after 5000 -> IO.puts("No response received")
end
```

In this example, the pid variable holds the PID of the spawned message handling process. The send/2 function is used to send a message to this PID, which includes the message itself and the PID of the sending process (self()). The receive/1 block captures the acknowledgment from the message handler.

Message Pattern Matching

One of the most powerful aspects of Elixir's message-passing model is the ability to use pattern matching within the receive/1 block. Processes can match specific patterns of incoming messages, allowing them to handle different message types.

Consider an extension of the previous example, where the MessageHandler can respond to different types of messages:

```
defmodule MessageHandler do
  def start do
    spawn(fn -> loop() end)
  end

  defp loop do
    receive do
      {sender, :ping} ->
        send(sender, {:ok, :pong})
        loop()

      {sender, :hello} ->
        send(sender, {:ok, "Hello there!"})
        loop()

      {sender, {:echo, message}} ->
        send(sender, {:ok, message})
        loop()
    end
  end
end
```

In this code, the loop/0 function handles three types of messages:

- A tuple containing the atom :ping, to which it responds with the atom :pong.
- A tuple containing the atom :hello, to which it responds with the string "Hello there!".
- A tuple containing another tuple :echo, message, to which it responds by echoing back the message.

Timeout in receive/1 Blocks

receive/1 blocks can also handle cases where no messages are received within a specific time frame. This is achieved using the after clause:

```
defmodule TimeoutHandler do
  def start do
    spawn(fn -> loop() end)
  end

  defp loop do
    receive do
      message ->
        IO.puts("Received message: #{message}")
        loop()
    after
      5000 ->
        IO.puts("No messages received within 5 seconds")
        loop()
    end
  end
end
```

In this example, the receive/1 block waits for messages but will output a timeout message if no message is received within 5 seconds. The process then continues running its loop/0 function.

Asynchronous vs. Synchronous Communication

Elixir's message passing is inherently asynchronous, meaning the sender does not wait for a response before continuing execution. However, it is possible to implement synchronous communication patterns by combining message passing with receive/1 blocks:

```
defmodule SyncHandler do
  def start do
    spawn(fn -> loop() end)
  end

  defp loop do
    receive do
      {sender, message} ->
        send(sender, {:ok, handle_message(message)})
        loop()
    end
  end

  defp handle_message(message), do: "Handled message: #{message}"
end
```

In this implementation, the sending process can request a response and wait synchronously:

```
pid = SyncHandler.start()
send(pid, {self(), "Sync test message"})

response = receive do
  {:ok, result} -> result
  after 5000 -> "No response received"
end
```

```
IO.puts(response)
```

Here, the sending process waits for a response before proceeding, ensuring synchronous communication through message passing.

The concepts of sending and receiving messages in Elixir lay the groundwork for building robust and flexible concurrent applications. Mastery of these techniques allows developers to harness the full power of the Erlang virtual machine (BEAM), upon which Elixir runs, fostering efficient and maintainable systems.

5.5 Process Lifecycle and Exit Signals

Understanding the lifecycle of processes and the signaling involved when a process exits is crucial for managing concurrency in Elixir effectively. Each process in Elixir operates independently, and processes communicate through message passing. Here, we elaborate on the birth, life, and termination of a process, and the signals exchanged during these phases.

At the heart of managing process lifecycles are the spawn/1, spawn/3, spawn_link/1, and spawn_link/3 functions. These functions allow the creation of new processes, but understanding their nuances provides better control over process behaviors and interprocess relationships.

The spawn function creates a new process and returns its Process ID (PID):

```
pid = spawn(fn -> perform_task() end)
```

The perform_task/0 function runs within the newly spawned process. This process operates concurrently with the parent process, and its lifecycle begins upon execution.

Processes can terminate due to normal completion or unexpected errors. The exit signals, such as :normal, :kill, and :shutdown, are of particular importance. These signals dictate how the termination impacts linked processes.

A process can terminate normally when it completes its task:

```
def perform_task do
  # Task execution logic
  :ok
end
```

Terminating with :ok ensures the process exits normally, which is typically harmless to other processes. An abnormal termination might occur due to an unhandled error:

```
def perform_task do
  raise "Unexpected error"
end
```

In this case, the process terminates with an error signal, impacting linked processes differently based on the signal type. Accidentally terminated processes emit :kill, an untrappable signal forcing termination. Conversely, a shutdown signal arises from orderly system shutdowns.

Linking processes with spawn_link/1 or spawn_link/3 ensures bidirectional connections:

```
pid = spawn_link(fn -> perform_task() end)
```

Linked processes impact each other's lifecycle. If one process terminates abnormally, its linked process(es) receive exit signals and potentially terminate too, ensuring failure propagation. However, managing these terminations intelligently is essential for system robustness.

Exit signals can be intercepted using trap exits, allowing processes to handle exit signals gracefully:

```
Process.flag(:trap_exit, true)
```

By enabling exit trapping, processes convert exit signals into regular messages:

```
def perform_task do
  receive do
    {:EXIT, _from, reason} -> IO.puts("Process exited with reason: #{reason}")
  end
  :ok
end
```

Linking and trapping exits aid in controlling process cleanup and system recovery after failures. Additionally, the :EXIT tuples help debug termination causes, enhancing fault tolerance strategies.

A practical process lifecycle management example involves a supervisor process monitoring worker processes:

```
def supervisor_loop do
  receive do
    {:EXIT, _pid, reason} ->
      IO.puts("Worker terminated: #{reason}")
      # Optionally restart worker
      spawn_link(fn -> worker_task() end)
  end
```

```
  supervisor_loop()
end
```

The supervisor process continuously monitors worker terminations and relaunches them, ensuring persistent availability.

Signals :normal, :shutdown, and :kill affect linked processes distinctively. Understanding their implications prevents cascading failures and enables refined error handling. Practitioners should use signals judiciously to maintain system stability.

In Elixir, constructing robust concurrent applications mandates adept process lifecycle management. Mastering exit signals and applying sophisticated process linking ensures resilient and reliable concurrent systems. This section consolidates fundamental aspects essential for expert proficiency in process-based Elixir applications.

5.6 Monitoring and Linking Processes

In concurrent systems built using the actor model, processes often need to be aware of the state and existence of other processes to maintain fault tolerance and resilience. Elixir provides two mechanisms for processes to monitor and link with one another: *monitoring* and *linking*. Both mechanisms offer ways to handle failures and to ensure that processes can recover gracefully from unexpected terminations.

Monitoring processes involves creating a unidirectional connection between two processes. The monitoring process receives a notification if the monitored process terminates, but the monitored process remains unaware of this relationship. This is useful for scenarios where a process needs to keep track of another process's status without direct interference.

To create a monitor, use the :erlang.monitor/2 function, which returns a reference that can be used later to identify the monitored process. Here's an illustrative example:

```
parent = self()
spawn(fn ->
  ref = :erlang.monitor(:process, parent)
  receive do
    {:DOWN, ^ref, :process, _pid, reason} ->
      IO.puts("The parent process has terminated with reason: #{reason}")
  end
end)
```

In this code, a child process monitors the parent process. If the parent process terminates, the child process will receive a :DOWN message containing the reference ref, indicating the termination reason.

The format of the :DOWN message is:

```
{:DOWN, ref, :process, pid, reason}
```

Where ref is the reference returned by :erlang.monitor/2, pid is the process identifier of the terminated process, and reason specifies why the process exited.

Linking processes, on the other hand, creates a bidirectional connection between processes. If either process terminates, the other process will receive an exit signal. This mechanism is useful in creating supervisee-supervisor relationships where the failure of one process necessitates the restart of another to maintain system consistency.

A process can be linked to another using the Process.link/1 function. Here is an example:

```
parent = self()
spawn_link(fn ->
  receive do
    {:EXIT, ^parent, reason} ->
      IO.puts("The parent process exited with reason: #{reason}")
  end
end)
```

In this example, the child process is linked to the parent process using spawn_link/1. If the parent process exits, the child process will receive an :EXIT message.

To gracefully exit a linked process without sending unnecessary exit signals, use Process.exit/2. Here's how to do it:

```
Process.exit(parent, :normal)
```

This function sends an exit signal to the specified process with the given reason (in this case, :normal). If the reason is :normal, the linked processes will not terminate, maintaining system stability.

Another powerful feature of Elixir is the ability to trap exits. By calling Process.flag/2 with the :trap_exit flag set to true, a process can convert exit signals into :EXIT messages that can be handled explicitly. Consider the following code:

```
parent = self()
Process.flag(:trap_exit, true)

spawn_link(fn ->
```

```
  exit(:error)
end)

receive do
  {:EXIT, _pid, reason} ->
    IO.puts("Received exit signal with reason: #{reason}")
end
```

In this scenario, the parent process sets the :trap_exit flag to true, converting any exit signals into :EXIT messages. When the child process terminates with an :error reason, the parent process receives and handles the :EXIT message.

Monitoring and linking provide robust mechanisms for fault tolerance in Elixir applications. Monitoring is non-intrusive and allows you to keep track of other processes, while linking ensures mutual awareness and dependency. By strategically using these tools, you can create resilient systems capable of recovering from process failures efficiently.

5.7 Task Module for Easier Concurrency

The Task module in Elixir provides a higher-level abstraction for creating and managing asynchronous tasks. It simplifies the implementation of concurrent code by offering a straightforward mechanism to spawn asynchronous processes and retrieve their results. The Task module is particularly useful for scenarios where you need to perform concurrent computations or IO-bound operations without dealing with the intricacies of process message-passing and process lifecycle management.

Task makes concurrency more accessible by abstracting away some of the lower-level details of process management. This facilitates easier development and maintenance of concurrent applications. Let us delve into the various functionalities of the Task module and how it can be employed to achieve efficient concurrency in Elixir.

```
iex> task = Task.async(fn -> heavy_computation() end)
%Task{...
```

The Task.async/1 function spawns a new process that executes the given function asynchronously. It returns a Task struct, which contains information about the task, including the PID of the spawned process.

Task.async/1 is useful when you want to offload a computationally expensive function to run concurrently without blocking the main process. Here, heavy_computation() represents a function that performs a resource-intensive operation.

To retrieve the result of the asynchronous task, use Task.await/1:

```
iex> Task.await(task)
:ok
```

Task.await/1 blocks the calling process until the result of the task is available or an optional timeout is reached. This function allows you to collect the result of the asynchronous computation once it completes.

Consider a more advanced usage scenario where multiple asynchronous tasks are spawned and their results are aggregated. For example, in an application that fetches data from multiple external APIs concurrently, you can utilize the Task module to manage these operations asynchronously.

```
def fetch_data_from_apis() do
  urls = ["http://api1.example.com", "http://api2.example.com", "http://api3.example.
      com"]
  tasks = Enum.map(urls, fn url -> Task.async(fn -> fetch_data(url) end) end)

  results = Enum.map(tasks, fn task -> Task.await(task) end)
  results
end

defp fetch_data(url) do
  # Simulate a network request
  :timer.sleep(1000)
  {:ok, "data from #{url}"}
end
```

In the above code snippet, the fetch_data_from_apis/0 function demonstrates how to leverage the Task module to fetch data simultaneously from multiple APIs. The Enum.map/2 function is used to create asynchronous tasks for each URL by calling Task.async/1 with the fetch_data/1 function. Subsequently, Task.await/1 is employed to block the calling process until all asynchronous tasks are completed and their results are collected. The fetch_data/1 function simulates a network request by using :timer.sleep/1, representing a delay indicative of an IO-bound operation.

For scenarios where you need to monitor or link tasks, the Task module provides additional functionalities. Tasks can be linked to the calling process to ensure that task failures are propagated. This can be achieved using Task.async/2 with an additional option to link the task:

```
task = Task.async(fn -> potentially_failing_operation() end, link: true)
begin
  result = Task.await(task)
  IO.puts("Operation successful: #{result}")
rescue
```

```
  Task.Supervisor, reason ->
    IO.puts("Operation failed: #{reason}")
end
```

In this example, potentially_failing_operation/0 is an operation that might fail. By linking the task, if the operation fails, the failure is propagated, and appropriate handling can be enacted using rescue. Task.await/1 retrieves the result, and if a failure occurs, it is caught and processed within the rescue block.

For cases that require dynamic supervision of tasks, the Task.Supervisor module can be leveraged. Task supervisors provide a way to dynamically manage and supervise a pool of tasks, ensuring they are correctly restarted when necessary:

```
def start_task_supervisor do
  Supervisor.start_link(
    [{Task.Supervisor, name: MyApp.TaskSupervisor}],
    strategy: :one_for_one
  )
end

def async_supervised_task(module, function, args) do
  Task.Supervisor.async_nolink(MyApp.TaskSupervisor, module, function, args)
end
```

In this scenario, Task.Supervisor is started within a supervision tree with a one_for_one strategy, meaning if a child task terminates abnormally, only that task is restarted. The async_supervised_task/3 function can then be utilized to start tasks under the supervision of MyApp.TaskSupervisor using Task.Supervisor.async_nolink/4.

Utilizing the Task module for concurrency in Elixir provides a powerful, yet simple means to manage asynchronous operations effectively. By abstracting away the lower-level details of process handling and lifecycle management, Elixir's Task module facilitates the development of reliable, concurrent applications. These capabilities are instrumental in building scalable applications that can efficiently handle multiple tasks concurrently while maintaining robustness and fault tolerance.

5.8 Handling State with Agents

In Elixir, an Agent is a specialized process designed to manage and encapsulate state. Agents simplify state management by providing functions to manipulate encapsulated state, thus abstracting away the complexities of direct process communication for stateful operations.

They are especially useful when you need a managed, long-lived state that can be accessed and updated by multiple parts of an application concurrently.

To create and manage Agents, Elixir provides the Agent module, which supports state initialization, synchronous and asynchronous state updates, and state retrieval. This section delves into the core functionalities of Agents, offering practical code examples to elucidate their operations.

```
# Start an Agent with an initial state of an empty list
{:ok, agent} = Agent.start(fn -> [] end)
```

The Agent.start/1 function initializes an Agent with the initial state set by the provided function. In this example, the anonymous function fn -> [] end initializes the state to an empty list. The function returns a tuple, where :ok indicates successful creation, and agent is the process identifier (PID) of the agent.

```
{:ok, #PID<0.123.0>}
```

To retrieve the state of an Agent, use the Agent.get/2 function. It accepts the Agent's PID and a function to be invoked on the state.

```
# Retrieve the current state of the Agent
state = Agent.get(agent, fn state -> state end)
```

Here, the function fn state -> state end simply returns the current state. The Agent.get/2 function ensures that this retrieval operation is synchronous.

In addition to state retrieval, Agents allow for synchronous and asynchronous state updates. Use the Agent.update/2 function for asynchronous updates and the Agent.get_and_update/2 function for synchronous updates where obtaining and modifying the state is necessary.

```
# Update the state to include a new element
:ok = Agent.update(agent, fn state -> ["new element" | state] end)
```

The above call prepends the string "new element" to the list maintained by the Agent. Notice that Agent.update/2 is asynchronous, meaning it will return immediately after initiating the update.

For cases where retrieving the current state and updating it should be atomic, use Agent.get_and_update/2.

```
# Retrieve the state and append a new element
new_state = Agent.get_and_update(agent, fn state -> {state, state ++ ["appended
```

```
    element"]} end)
```

This function returns the original state and updates it by appending "appended element" to the list, ensuring that both operations occur atomically.

Agents also support more complex state manipulations via functions like Agent.cast/2 for fire-and-forget updates and Agent.stop/2 to terminate the Agent process.

```
# Stop the Agent
:ok = Agent.stop(agent)
```

This call graciously terminates the Agent, allowing for any necessary cleanup.

```
:ok
```

Agents in Elixir present an idiomatic approach to managing state with minimal boilerplate code. They integrate seamlessly with the actor model philosophy of Elixir, keeping state encapsulated within processes while providing straightforward functions to manipulate that state.

The combination of synchronous and asynchronous operations allows for flexible and efficient state management, making Agents a powerful tool in the Elixir developer's toolkit.

5.9 Building a Simple Process-Based Application

Building process-based applications in Elixir offers a practical perspective on leveraging concurrency effectively. This section demonstrates building a simple chat server application, illustrating the concepts discussed in the preceding sections. The chat server will handle multiple clients, allowing them to join, leave, and exchange messages in real-time.

To begin, we need a module to handle the logic of our chat server:

```
defmodule ChatServer do
  def start_link do
    spawn_link(__MODULE__, :init, [])
  end

  def init do
    loop(%{})
```

```
  end

  defp loop(clients) do
    receive do
      {:join, pid, name} ->
        new_clients = Map.put(clients, pid, name)
        notify_all(new_clients, "#{name} has joined the chat")
        loop(new_clients)
      {:leave, pid} ->
        name = Map.get(clients, pid)
        new_clients = Map.delete(clients, pid)
        notify_all(new_clients, "#{name} has left the chat")
        loop(new_clients)
      {:message, from_pid, message} ->
        name = Map.get(clients, from_pid)
        notify_all(clients, "[#{name}]: #{message}")
        loop(clients)
    end
  end

  defp notify_all(clients, message) do
    Enum.each(clients, fn {pid, _name} ->
      send(pid, {:chat_message, message})
    end)
  end
end
```

The ChatServer module defines the main server logic. The start_link/0 function spawns a new process linked to the current process, ensuring it will be terminated if the parent process dies. The init/0 function initializes the server state as an empty map, representing connected clients. The core of the logic resides within the loop/1 function, which continuously handles incoming messages:

- When a client joins, the server updates the client list and notifies everyone.
- When a client leaves, the server removes the client from the list and broadcasts a leave message.
- When a message is received, it is broadcast to all clients.

The notify_all/2 function is a helper function to send a message to all connected clients.

Next, we need a module representing the clients:

```
defmodule ChatClient do
  def start(name, server_pid) do
    spawn(fn -> init(name, server_pid) end)
  end

  defp init(name, server_pid) do
    send(server_pid, {:join, self(), name})
```

```
    loop(server_pid)
  end

  defp loop(server_pid) do
    receive do
      {:chat_message, message} ->
        IO.puts(message)
        loop(server_pid)
    end
  end

  def send_message(pid, message) do
    send(pid, {:message, self(), message})
  end

  def leave(pid) do
    send(pid, {:leave, self()})
  end
end
```

The ChatClient module encapsulates the client-side logic. The start/2 function spawns a new client process. The init/2 function sends a join message to the server. The heart of the client logic resides in the loop/1 function:

- When a :chat_message is received, it prints the message to the console.

Additionally, the send_message/2 function allows clients to send messages to the server, whereas the leave/1 function enables them to leave the chat.

Finally, let's demonstrate how to use these modules by creating a simple usage example:

```
defmodule ChatDemo do
  def run do
    server_pid = ChatServer.start_link()
    client1 = ChatClient.start("Alice", server_pid)
    client2 = ChatClient.start("Bob", server_pid)

    Process.send_after(client1, {:message, self(), "Hello everyone!"}, 1000)
    Process.send_after(client2, {:message, self(), "Hi Alice!"}, 2000)
    Process.send_after(client1, {:leave, self()}, 3000)

    :timer.sleep(4000)
  end
end

ChatDemo.run()
```

In this example, we create a module ChatDemo to encapsulate our demo logic. The run/0 function starts the chat server and spawns two clients, Alice and Bob. Using Process.send_after/3, we automate sending messages and leaving the chat for demonstration purposes. Finally, we halt for 4 seconds to allow asynchronous activities to complete before the script ends.

```
Alice has joined the chat
Bob has joined the chat
[Bob]: Hi Alice!
Alice has left the chat
```

This simple application demonstrates the power of the actor model and process-based concurrency in Elixir. By leveraging processes and message passing, we achieve a lightweight, scalable, fault-tolerant architecture for concurrent tasks.

Chapter 6

OTP: Design Principles and Behaviors

This chapter provides an in-depth look at the Open Telecom Platform (OTP) in Elixir. It covers the core components including GenServer, Supervisors, and Supervision Trees, as well as application behaviors and design principles. Examining OTP behaviors such as GenEvent and GenFSM, the chapter also discusses supervision strategies, dynamic supervision, and process registration using the Registry. A hands-on example guides the application of these concepts in a practical context.

6.1 Introduction to OTP

The Open Telecom Platform (OTP) provides a powerful framework for building robust, scalable, and maintainable applications in Elixir. OTP is a set of libraries and design principles that extend the capabilities of the Erlang runtime system, on which Elixir runs. Understanding OTP is crucial for maximizing the potential of Elixir in both simple and complex applications.

OTP offers several core components, including GenServer, Supervisors, Supervision Trees, and various behaviors. Each of these components enhances the functionality of Elixir applications by offering tested and standardized approaches to common programming challenges. By leveraging OTP, developers can build fault-tolerant systems that can self-heal and manage unexpected conditions gracefully.

Key Concepts of OTP OTP introduces several behaviors that encapsulate common patterns used in concurrent programming. The most fundamental ones are:

- GenServer
- Supervisors
- Applications

Each of these plays a specialized role in designing and maintaining an Elixir application.

GenServer is an abstraction layer that simplifies implementing the server of a client-server relationship. It manages state, handles synchronous and asynchronous calls, and provides a clean way to encapsulate and reuse functionality.

```
defmodule MyServer do
  use GenServer

  # Client API

  def start_link(init_arg) do
    GenServer.start_link(__MODULE__, init_arg, name: __MODULE__)
  end

  def get_state do
    GenServer.call(__MODULE__, :get_state)
  end

  # Server Callbacks

  @impl true
  def init(init_arg) do
    {:ok, init_arg}
  end

  @impl true
  def handle_call(:get_state, _from, state) do
    {:reply, state, state}
  end
end
```

In the example above, MyServer implements a GenServer that initializes with a given argument and can respond to synchronous calls asking for its state.

Supervisors are special processes designed to monitor and manage other processes, which are referred to as worker processes. Supervisors can automatically restart child processes if they fail, providing a foundation for building fault-tolerant systems. They support various strategies for managing child processes, such as *one-for-one*, *one-for-all*, and *rest-for-one*.

```
defmodule MySupervisor do
  use Supervisor

  def start_link(init_arg) do
    Supervisor.start_link(__MODULE__, init_arg, name: __MODULE__)
  end

  @impl true
  def init(_init_arg) do
    children = [
      {MyServer, "initial_state"}
    ]

    Supervisor.init(children, strategy: :one_for_one)
  end
end
```

This example sets up a Supervisor that starts MyServer with an initial state. The one_for_one strategy ensures that if MyServer crashes, it will be restarted without affecting other child processes.

Applications encapsulate an entire running system, coordinating the starting and stopping of all necessary components. They follow a specific structure and lifecycle defined by OTP, which includes specifying the application's supervision tree.

```
defmodule MyApp.Application do
  use Application

  @impl true
  def start(_type, _args) do
    children = [
      MySupervisor
    ]

    opts = [strategy: :one_for_one, name: MyApp.Supervisor]
    Supervisor.start_link(children, opts)
  end
end
```

The MyApp.Application module demonstrates how an OTP application is defined. It includes a start/2 function that initializes the supervision tree for the application using MySupervisor.

These components combined create a robust framework that allows developers to build resilient systems. OTP provides standardized solutions for managing concurrency, process lifecycle, and fault tolerance, which are essential in modern applications.

To delve deeper into OTP, it's important to understand not only the individual behaviors like GenServer and Supervisors but also how they interact and complement each other within the system. The subsequent sections of this chapter will explore these concepts, their implementations, and their interactions in more detail.

6.2 GenServer: The Backbone of Elixir Applications

In Elixir, a GenServer (short for Generic Server) is an abstraction that facilitates the implementation of server processes adhering to the OTP design principles. A GenServer enables developers to create and manage concurrent processes with ease, making it a cornerstone of robust, concurrent applications.

A GenServer has a well-defined lifecycle consisting of callbacks that handle initialization, termination, message processing, and state management. These callbacks, generally implemented as part of a module using the GenServer behavior, make it possible to build reliable and maintainable parts of an application.

Initialization

The initialization of a GenServer is managed via the init/1 callback. This callback is invoked when the server is started, and it sets the initial state of the server. The init/1 function returns a tuple, typically {:ok, State} where State refers to the initial state of the GenServer.

```
defmodule MyGenServer do
  use GenServer

  def init(initial_state) do
    {:ok, initial_state}
  end
end
```

Synchronous Requests: call/2

Synchronous requests are handled using the handle_call/3 callback. This callback processes incoming call/2 requests, which block the calling process until a reply is received from the GenServer. The handle_call/3 function usually returns a tuple {:reply, Reply, NewState}, where Reply is sent back to the caller and NewState is the updated state of the server.

```
defmodule MyGenServer do
  use GenServer
```

```
  # Client API
  def get_state(pid) do
    GenServer.call(pid, :get_state)
  end

  # Server Callbacks
  def handle_call(:get_state, _from, state) do
    {:reply, state, state}
  end
end
```

```
iex> {:ok, pid} = GenServer.start_link(MyGenServer, :initial_state)
iex> MyGenServer.get_state(pid)
:initial_state
```

Asynchronous Requests: cast/2

In contrast, asynchronous requests are managed using the handle_cast/2 callback. These requests do not block the calling process, enabling it to continue executing other code while the server processes the request. The handle_cast/2 function returns a tuple {:noreply, NewState} indicating no immediate reply is sent to the caller.

```
defmodule MyGenServer do
  use GenServer

  # Client API
  def set_state(pid, new_state) do
    GenServer.cast(pid, {:set_state, new_state})
  end

  # Server Callbacks
  def handle_cast({:set_state, new_state}, _old_state) do
    {:noreply, new_state}
  end
end
```

```
iex> {:ok, pid} = GenServer.start_link(MyGenServer, :old_state)
iex> MyGenServer.set_state(pid, :new_state)
```

State Management and Code Organization

Proper state management is crucial in GenServers since each server maintains its own isolated state. This encapsulation allows for the modeling of resources such as database connections, caches, or any other stateful component.

For clarity, organizing the client API and server callbacks within a GenServer module is considered good practice. This separation aids in readability and maintainability, making the module easier to understand.

Termination

Handled via the terminate/2 callback, termination cleanup ensures resources are freed and consistent states are maintained. The terminate/2 function is called whenever a GenServer terminates, receiving the reason for shutdown and the current state.

```
defmodule MyGenServer do
  use GenServer

  def terminate(_reason, _state) do
    :ok
  end
end
```

Putting It All Together

A comprehensive example demonstrates the integration of call/2, cast/2, and lifecycle callbacks. Below is a complete GenServer module managing a counter state:

```
defmodule Counter do
  use GenServer

  # Client Functions
  def start_link(initial_value) do
    GenServer.start_link(__MODULE__, initial_value, name: __MODULE__)
  end

  def increment do
    GenServer.cast(__MODULE__, :increment)
  end

  def value do
    GenServer.call(__MODULE__, :value)
  end

  # Server Callbacks
  def init(initial_value) do
    {:ok, initial_value}
  end

  def handle_cast(:increment, state) do
    {:noreply, state + 1}
  end

  def handle_call(:value, _from, state) do
    {:reply, state, state}
  end

  def terminate(_reason, _state) do
    :ok
  end
end
```

```
iex> Counter.start_link(0)
iex> Counter.increment()
iex> Counter.value()
```

1

6.3 Supervisors and Supervision Trees

Supervisors are fundamental components in the OTP (Open Telecom Platform) framework, central to building fault-tolerant applications in Elixir. They manage other processes, termed child processes, ensuring they are correctly started and remain operational. When these child processes terminate unexpectedly, Supervisors can restart them according to predefined strategies, thereby adhering to the "let it crash" philosophy, which simplifies error handling and increases system resilience.

Supervision trees are hierarchical structures comprising multiple Supervisors and workers (i.e., processes performing the actual work tasks like GenServer processes). Each Supervisor can have multiple children, which can be either workers or other Supervisors, leading to nested supervision structures that enable complex applications to recover from failure states at various levels.

A Supervisor's behavior is configured via a child_spec, typically defined in the child module, specifying key parameters like the module to start, the start function and its arguments, restart strategy, number of retries, and the maximum time frame for these retries. Below is an example defining a simple child_spec for a module named MyWorker:

```
defmodule MyWorker do
  use GenServer

  ## Callbacks

  def init(args) do
    {:ok, args}
  end

  # Other GenServer callback functions

  def child_spec(opts) do
    %{
      id: __MODULE__,
      start: {__MODULE__, :start_link, [opts]},
      type: :worker,
      restart: :permanent
    }
  end
end
```

In the Supervisors module, the children are specified in a list passed to the Supervisor's init function. The children's specification includes their respective child_specs, defining how they should be started and monitored.

```
defmodule MySupervisor do
  use Supervisor

  def start_link(init_arg) do
    Supervisor.start_link(__MODULE__, init_arg, name: __MODULE__)
  end

  def init(_init_arg) do
    children = [
      MyWorker.child_spec(arg1)
      # Add more children here
    ]

    Supervisor.init(children, strategy: :one_for_one)
  end
end
```

The strategy option in the Supervisor's init function determines the restart behavior upon child process termination. There are four primary strategies:

- :one_for_one - Restart only the terminated child process. This is the most common strategy.
- :one_for_all - Restart all child processes if one child process terminates. This strategy ensures that all processes are always started with a consistent state.
- :rest_for_one - Restart the terminated child and any children started after it. Useful when later processes depend on the earlier ones.
- :simple_one_for_one - Similar to one_for_one but optimized for dynamically adding and removing children, typical in scenarios like dynamic worker pools.

Supervision trees become increasingly complex as applications grow. Nested supervisors are employed to encapsulate distinct parts of the system, allowing targeted recovery from failures. For example, a real-world application might use a combination of all strategies in various parts of the tree.

Below is an example of a more complex supervision tree where 'MyWorker' and another worker 'AnotherWorker' are supervised by 'MySupervisor', and 'MySupervisor' itself is supervised by a root supervisor:

```
defmodule RootSupervisor do
  use Supervisor

  def start_link(init_arg) do
    Supervisor.start_link(__MODULE__, init_arg, name: __MODULE__)
  end

  def init(_init_arg) do
    children = [
      {MySupervisor, arg1},
      {AnotherWorker, arg2}
    ]

    Supervisor.init(children, strategy: :one_for_one)
  end
end
```

In this example, AnotherWorker is directly supervised by RootSupervisor, while MyWorker is indirectly supervised through MySupervisor.

Key to designing effective supervision trees is balancing fault tolerance and performance. While having many nested Supervisors can increase system resilience by isolating failure domains, it can also introduce overhead and complexity. The decision of how deep and broad the supervision tree should be depends on the specific requirements and characteristics of the application being developed.

Additionally, all child processes, be they workers or Supervisors, should have well-defined child_specs, ensuring their life cycle is managed uniformly. This standard structuring simplifies the dynamic addition, removal, or reallocation of processes within the supervision tree based on real-time requirements.

To dynamically manage child processes, the DynamicSupervisor module is employed. It offers a flexible mechanism to add and remove children in response to runtime conditions, expanding the static nature of traditional supervision trees:

```
defmodule MyDynamicSupervisor do
  use DynamicSupervisor

  def start_link(init_arg) do
    DynamicSupervisor.start_link(__MODULE__, init_arg, name: __MODULE__)
  end

  def init(_init_arg) do
    DynamicSupervisor.init(strategy: :one_for_one)
  end

  def start_child(worker_args) do
    spec = {MyWorker, worker_args}
    DynamicSupervisor.start_child(__MODULE__, spec)
  end
```

```
  def terminate_child(pid) do
    DynamicSupervisor.terminate_child(__MODULE__, pid)
  end
end
```

This approach is particularly beneficial for scenarios requiring high scalability and flexibility, such as task queues or pool management systems.

By structuring applications with Supervisors and Supervision Trees, developers can create robust, fault-tolerant systems capable of self-healing and maintaining consistent performance even under failure conditions. Embracing these robust design patterns is essential for developing resilient Elixir applications.

6.4 Applications and Application Behaviors

Understanding OTP (Open Telecom Platform) applications and their behaviors is essential for building robust and scalable systems in Elixir. OTP applications serve as the fundamental building blocks of Elixir-based systems, encapsulating all components and logic necessary for their functioning. In this section, we will explore the key concepts, components, and behaviors associated with OTP applications.

An OTP application is essentially a component that can be started and stopped as a unit, and typically includes components such as supervisors and worker processes. These applications facilitate the management of application lifecycle through standardization of start, stop, and configuration mechanisms, promoting code reuse and robustness.

To define an OTP application, the mix build tool in Elixir provides a straightforward mechanism. Let's start by generating a new application using the mix command:

```
$ mix new my_app --app my_app
```

This command creates the basic structure including a mix.exs file that configures the application. The primary configuration inside the mix.exs file encompasses the application specification, defining the modules to start, application's dependencies, and versioning. Here is an example of what the mix.exs file looks like:

```
defmodule MyApp.MixProject do
  use Mix.Project

  def project do
```

```
    [
      app: :my_app,
      version: "0.1.0",
      elixir: "~> 1.11",
      start_permanent: Mix.env() == :prod,
      deps: deps()
    ]
  end

  def application do
    [
      extra_applications: [:logger],
      mod: {MyApp.Application, []}
    ]
  end

  defp deps do
    []
  end
end
```

The application/0 function inside mix.exs specifies the applications and modules to be managed by OTP. Here, the mod key contains a tuple where the first element is the application callback module (MyApp.Application). The second element is an argument list to be passed to the start/2 callback function of this module.

We define the MyApp.Application module to implement the Application behavior. Below is a basic example of this module:

```
defmodule MyApp.Application do
  use Application

  def start(_type, _args) do
    children = [
      %{
        id: MyApp.Worker,
        start: {MyApp.Worker, :start_link, []}
      }
    ]

    opts = [strategy: :one_for_one, name: MyApp.Supervisor]
    Supervisor.start_link(children, opts)
  end
end
```

Here, the start/2 callback initializes the application's supervision tree. The children list defines the worker processes and supervisors to be started. The opts specifies supervision strategy; {:one_for_one} indicates that if a worker process crashes, the supervisor restarts only that crashed process.

In Elixir, applications are typically structured using behaviors. OTP behaviors such as Application and Supervisor provide predefined linkage to callbacks that allow specific implementations. Implementing these behaviors ensures standardization and facilitates extensibility.

Let's break down the start/2 callback of the MyApp.Application module. The callback takes two arguments, _type and _args, ignoring them as denoted by the _ prefix, a common convention in Elixir to signal unused variables. The children list specifies the worker processes and involves specifying the module (MyApp.Worker), the start function (:start_link), and the arguments (empty list in this case).

Next, consider the MyApp.Worker module, a simple GenServer:

```
defmodule MyApp.Worker do
  use GenServer

  def start_link(_) do
    GenServer.start_link(__MODULE__, %{}, name: __MODULE__)
  end

  def init(state) do
    {:ok, state}
  end
end
```

A GenServer behavior is leveraged here by calling use GenServer, providing a set of default implementations and callbacks. The start_link/1 function is responsible for initiating the GenServer process, and init/1 sets the initial state, returning a tuple with the atom :ok and the initial state.

Another important aspect of OTP applications is handling application configurations. Elixir provides comprehensive support for fetching and managing configurations using Application.get_env/3 and Application.put_env/4. The application's configuration can be specified in config/config.exs:

```
use Mix.Config

config :my_app, key: :value
```

Understanding and implementing OTP applications and their behaviors is paramount. Through this standardization, OTP lays the foundation for building scalable, maintainable, and resilient systems in Elixir.

6.5 Building a GenServer from Scratch

In this section, we will delve into the process of building a GenServer from scratch. The GenServer module provides a standard set of functions for implementing server processes. This abstraction simplifies the creation of servers that handle synchronous and asynchronous requests and manage state effectively.

We will create a GenServer that manages a simple key-value store. This will involve initializing state, handling synchronous calls, managing asynchronous requests, and implementing termination logic. The complete implementation will clarify how GenServer leverages the OTP framework to provide robustness and fault-tolerance.

Start by creating a new module named KVStore. Define this module and use GenServer to specify that this module will implement the GenServer behavior.

```
defmodule KVStore do
  use GenServer

  # Interface functions

  def start_link(initial_state \\ %{}) do
    GenServer.start_link(__MODULE__, initial_state, name: __MODULE__)
  end

  def get(key) do
    GenServer.call(__MODULE__, {:get, key})
  end

  def put(key, value) do
    GenServer.cast(__MODULE__, {:put, key, value})
  end
end
```

The start_link/1 function initializes the GenServer, optionally accepting an initial state. It uses GenServer.start_link/3 to start the GenServer and register it with a name. The get/1 function interfaces synchronously with the GenServer through GenServer.call/2, while put/2 communicates asynchronously via GenServer.cast/2.

Next, implement the GenServer callbacks: init/1, handle_call/3, handle_cast/2, and terminate/2.

```
defmodule KVStore do
  use GenServer

  def start_link(initial_state \\ %{}) do
    GenServer.start_link(__MODULE__, initial_state, name: __MODULE__)
  end

  def get(key) do
    GenServer.call(__MODULE__, {:get, key})
  end

  def put(key, value) do
    GenServer.cast(__MODULE__, {:put, key, value})
  end
```

```
# GenServer callbacks

  @impl true
  def init(initial_state) do
    {:ok, initial_state}
  end

  @impl true
  def handle_call({:get, key}, _from, state) do
    value = Map.get(state, key, :not_found)
    {:reply, value, state}
  end

  @impl true
  def handle_cast({:put, key, value}, state) do
    new_state = Map.put(state, key, value)
    {:noreply, new_state}
  end

  @impl true
  def terminate(_reason, _state) do
    :ok
  end
end
```

The init/1 callback initializes the GenServer's state. The handle_call/3 function processes synchronous calls, extracting the key and searching the state map. It responds with the found value or :not_found. The handle_cast/2 function handles asynchronous requests, inserting or updating the key-value pair in the state map. The terminate/2 callback ensures proper cleanup upon server termination.

To utilize this GenServer, start by adding KVStore to your application's supervision tree. Assuming an existing application module, modify the children list in the start/2 function to include KVStore.

```
defmodule MyApp.Application do
  use Application

  def start(_type, _args) do
    children = [
      KVStore
    ]

    opts = [strategy: :one_for_one, name: MyApp.Supervisor]
    Supervisor.start_link(children, opts)
  end
end
```

Running MyApp.Application will now start the KVStore GenServer as part of the application's supervision tree, ensuring it benefits from the resilience provided by OTP.

Utilize the KVStore in the following manner:

```
iex> KVStore.start_link()
```

```
{:ok, #PID<0.215.0>}

iex> KVStore.put(:foo, "bar")
:ok

iex> KVStore.get(:foo)
"bar"

iex> KVStore.get(:non_existent_key)
:not_found
```

This sequence confirms the proper functioning of our custom GenServer. The put/2 function asynchronously updates the state, while get/1 retrieves values synchronously, demonstrating the key-value storage capabilities.

A comprehensive GenServer must handle various edge cases and potential failures. Consider adding logic for error handling, timeouts, and state persistence to enhance robustness further. These additions are critical for production systems where reliability and fault-tolerance are paramount.

Refining and expanding on this foundation with advanced patterns and practices will solidify understanding and proficiency in developing robust, scalable applications with OTP and GenServer. The principles demonstrated here form the bedrock upon which more complex systems are constructed, illustrating the power and elegance of Elixir's concurrency model.

6.6 Using OTP Behaviors: GenEvent, GenFSM, etc.

Open Telecom Platform (OTP) provides various behaviors to standardize the construction of robust and fault-tolerant applications. Among the key behaviors provided by OTP, GenEvent and GenFSM play crucial roles in building flexible, event-driven systems and finite state machines, respectively. Understanding and leveraging these behaviors can significantly enhance the robustness and maintainability of Elixir applications.

GenEvent is an event manager that allows the addition and removal of event handling modules dynamically. It serves as a mediator where events are sent to and distributed among multiple handlers. Handlers can be attached and detached at runtime, making GenEvent a powerful tool for building extensible systems.

To create a GenEvent manager and attach handlers, the following steps are usually followed:

```
defmodule MyApp.EventHandler do
  use GenEvent

  def handle_event(event, state) do
    IO.puts("Handling event: #{event}")
    {:ok, state}
  end
end

{:ok, manager} = GenEvent.start_link([])
GenEvent.add_handler(manager, MyApp.EventHandler, [])
GenEvent.notify(manager, :some_event)
```

In this example, MyApp.EventHandler is a module that uses the GenEvent behavior. The handle_event/2 callback is implemented to define how events are processed. The start_link/1 function starts an event manager, and the add_handler/3 function attaches the event handler to this manager. Finally, the notify/2 function dispatches an event to the attached handlers.

GenFSM is another essential behavior for implementing finite state machines. Finite state machines (FSMs) are models of computation based on a finite number of states, transitions between those states, and actions. They are particularly useful in telecommunications and protocol implementation.

Here is an example of a simple GenFSM implementation:

```
defmodule MyApp.FSM do
  use GenFSM, initial_state: :state1

  def initial_state(:state1, data) do
    {:ok, :state1, data}
  end

  def state1(:event, data) do
    {:next_state, :state2, data}
  end

  def state2(:event, data) do
    {:next_state, :state1, data}
  end
end

{:ok, fsm} = GenFSM.start_link(MyApp.FSM, :initial_data)
GenFSM.send_event(fsm, :event)
```

In this example, MyApp.FSM is a module that uses the GenFSM behavior with an initial state of state1. The initial_state/2 function sets up the FSM's initial state, while state1/2 and state2/2 define the state transitions. Each state function returns a tuple indicating the next state and updated data. The send_event/2 function transitions the FSM based on events.

OTP also provides more specialized behaviors such as gen_statem, which is an update to GenFSM but offers more flexibility and better performance characteristics for complex state machines by supporting various kinds of state transitions like next events and deferred events.

Additionally, while working with these behaviors, it is crucial to understand supervision and fault tolerance. Supervisors monitor these processes and can restart them in case of failures. Combining OTP behaviors with appropriate supervision strategies ensures that systems can recover gracefully from unexpected conditions.

The DynamicSupervisor is another advanced feature of OTP that allows for dynamic addition and removal of child processes. This is particularly useful for use cases where the number of supervised processes cannot be determined at compile-time and needs to be managed dynamically at runtime.

Here is an example of using DynamicSupervisor:

```
defmodule MyApp.DynamicSupervisor do
  use DynamicSupervisor

  def start_link(init_arg) do
    DynamicSupervisor.start_link(__MODULE__, init_arg, name: __MODULE__)
  end

  def init(_init_arg) do
    DynamicSupervisor.init(strategy: :one_for_one)
  end

  def start_child(child_spec) do
    DynamicSupervisor.start_child(__MODULE__, child_spec)
  end
end

child_spec = %{id: MyWorker, start: {MyWorker, :start_link, []}}

MyApp.DynamicSupervisor.start_link(:ok)
MyApp.DynamicSupervisor.start_child(child_spec)
```

In this code, MyApp.DynamicSupervisor defines a dynamic supervisor using the DynamicSupervisor behavior. The start_child/2 function starts a new child process based on the provided child specification.

These OTP behaviors, when used effectively, enable developers to build robust, maintainable, and scalable applications by leveraging the power of concurrent processes, dynamic process management, and fault tolerance mechanisms provided by the OTP framework.

6.7 Supervision Strategies and Restart Policies

In OTP, one of the cornerstones ensuring robustness and fault tolerance of Elixir applications is the supervisor. Supervisors are specialized processes dedicated to monitoring one or more worker processes, referred to as children. The supervisor's main role is to apply specific strategies to restart child processes upon their failure, thus maintaining the system's resilience. This section meticulously explores various supervision strategies and restart policies.

Supervisors utilize predefined strategies to handle child process terminations. These strategies determine if and how child processes are restarted. To define a supervisor, we typically use the Supervisor module. Below is a fundamental structure of a supervisor initialization:

```
defmodule MyApp.Supervisor do
  use Supervisor

  def start_link(init_arg) do
    Supervisor.start_link(__MODULE__, init_arg, name: __MODULE__)
  end

  def init(_init_arg) do
    children = [
      %{
        id: MyServer,
        start: {MyServer, :start_link, []},
        restart: :permanent,
        shutdown: 5000,
        type: :worker
      }
    ]

    Supervisor.init(children, strategy: :one_for_one)
  end
end
```

Supervisor.start_link/2 function is called to initiate the supervisor process that will manage its children as defined in the init/1 callback. Here, the child specification for a worker module MyServer is outlined, including the intended restart policy.

There are four primary supervision strategies within OTP:

- :one_for_one
- :one_for_all
- :rest_for_one

- :simple_one_for_one

Each of these strategies tackles child failures distinctively.

:one_for_one:

This strategy ensures that only the terminated child process is restarted. Consider it for systems where child processes operate independently. It is denoted as:

```
Supervisor.init(children, strategy: :one_for_one)
```

For example, if MyServer crashes, the supervisor will restart only MyServer without affecting other child processes.

:one_for_all:

In this strategy, if any child process terminates, all other child processes are terminated and subsequently restarted. This approach is suitable when child processes depend critically on one another's state. The initialization syntax is as follows:

```
Supervisor.init(children, strategy: :one_for_all)
```

An example scenario includes a system where multiple worker processes must share a consistent data state; if one fails, the integrity of the others might necessitate a restart.

:rest_for_one:

With :rest_for_one, if a child process terminates, it and all subsequent child processes, as defined in the supervisor's child list, are terminated and restarted. This strategy is advantageous when child processes form a chain of dependencies. The corresponding initialization looks like:

```
Supervisor.init(children, strategy: :rest_for_one)
```

For instance, in a scenario where a primary process spawns secondary processes relying on its ongoing state, a failure in the primary would necessitate restarting the secondary processes as well.

:simple_one_for_one:

This strategy is a specialised version of :one_for_one, primarily used when managing dynamic number of similar child processes. It is often leveraged for handling dynamic worker pools. An example configuration would be:

```
Supervisor.init([MyChildSpec], strategy: :simple_one_for_one)
```

Here, the supervisor starts with no children and dynamically adds children processes as required through calls to Supervisor.start_child/2.

Key to understanding strategies is also grasping restart policies, which define under what conditions a child should be restarted:

- :permanent
- :temporary
- :transient

:permanent:

A permanent child process is always restarted irrespective of the reason for termination (normal, abnormal, or shutdown).

:temporary:

A temporary child process is never restarted, regardless of its termination cause. Use this policy for processes whose normal termination should not trigger a restart.

:transient:

A transient child process is only restarted if it terminates abnormally. If it exits normally or due to being intentionally shut down, it is not restarted.

Restart frequency and intensity, defined by max_restarts and max_-seconds, control excessive termination handling:

```
Supervisor.init(children, strategy: :one_for_one, max_restarts: 3, max_seconds: 5)
```

This configuration permits a maximum of three restarts within a five-second window before the supervisor itself terminates, potentially prompting a higher-level supervisor to take further action.

Understanding these supervision strategies and restart policies is pivotal, ensuring that an Elixir application demonstrates resilience and fault tolerance by correctly managing child process lifecycles and dependencies. This section has provided a detailed foundation for creating robust supervision trees and handling process failures effectively, contributing significantly to the reliability of systems built using Elixir.

6.8 Dynamic Supervision with DynamicSupervisor

Dynamic supervision in Elixir is primarily managed using the DynamicSupervisor module. It provides a mechanism for starting and terminating child processes dynamically, which is crucial for applications that require flexible process management. Unlike Supervisor, which starts all its children during initialization, DynamicSupervisor can start child processes on-the-fly as per varying runtime requirements.

The DynamicSupervisor is part of the Open Telecom Platform (OTP) framework and is designed to cater to scenarios where the number of child processes is not constant, and children need to be added or removed dynamically. This makes it ideal for applications such as web servers managing connections, real-time systems responding to fluctuating load, and other use cases requiring robust, adaptable process supervision.

Here, we'll delve into how to set up and utilize DynamicSupervisor effectively in an Elixir environment, followed by an example illustrating its practical application.

```
# Example of a simple worker module to be supervised dynamically
defmodule MyApp.Worker do
  use GenServer

  def start_link(arg) do
    GenServer.start_link(__MODULE__, arg, name: __MODULE__)
  end

  def init(initial_arg) do
    {:ok, initial_arg}
  end

  # Placeholder for handling GenServer callbacks
end
```

To utilize the DynamicSupervisor, it is necessary to define it within the supervision tree of your application. The DynamicSupervisor itself must be specified as a child of a static supervisor. This hierarchical setup allows for dynamic addition and removal of supervised processes under the DynamicSupervisor, while still ensuring the structure and restart capabilities provided by the static supervisor.

```
# Setting up the DynamicSupervisor in the supervision tree
defmodule MyApp.Application do
  use Application

  def start(_type, _args) do
```

```
    children = [
      {DynamicSupervisor, strategy: :one_for_one, name: MyApp.DynamicSupervisor}
    ]

    # Initializing the supervisor with the specified children
    opts = [strategy: :one_for_one, name: MyApp.Supervisor]
    Supervisor.start_link(children, opts)
  end
end
```

The DynamicSupervisor is initialized with a supervision strategy. Here, :one_for_one indicates that if a child process terminates, only that process is restarted. Other strategies include :one_for_all and :rest_for_one, analogous to those used by static supervisors.

Once the DynamicSupervisor is incorporated into your application's supervision tree, you can dynamically add children. This is achieved through the DynamicSupervisor.start_child/2 function, which allows you to specify the module and arguments needed to start the child process.

```
# Adding a worker dynamically
defmodule MyApp.WorkerManager do
  def start_worker(arg) do
    spec = {MyApp.Worker, arg}
    DynamicSupervisor.start_child(MyApp.DynamicSupervisor, spec)
  end

  def terminate_worker(pid) do
    DynamicSupervisor.terminate_child(MyApp.DynamicSupervisor, pid)
  end
end
```

In this example, MyApp.WorkerManager is responsible for dynamically starting and stopping worker processes. It uses the DynamicSupervisor.start_child/2 function to start a new worker with the given argument. Conversely, DynamicSupervisor.terminate_child/2 terminates a worker process, ensuring that child processes can be removed as needed.

Here is an example workflow demonstrating the interaction between a client request and the dynamic supervisor.

```
# Sample client module interacting with DynamicSupervisor
defmodule MyApp.Client do
  def new_worker_request(arg) do
    case MyApp.WorkerManager.start_worker(arg) do
      {:ok, pid} ->
        IO.puts("Worker started successfully with PID #{inspect(pid)}")
      {:error, reason} ->
        IO.puts("Failed to start worker: #{inspect(reason)}")
    end
  end
end
```

This client module would invoke new_worker_request/1 to start a new worker. The supervisor handles the instantiation and monitoring of the worker process. This interaction pattern allows the system to robustly respond to varied and unpredictable workloads dynamically.

When designing systems using DynamicSupervisor, it is critical to consider the potential resource constraints and implement strategies to handle scenarios where resource limits might be reached. Proper error handling and monitoring mechanisms should be in place to gracefully degrade service quality or reallocate resources as needed.

To summarize, DynamicSupervisor empowers Elixir applications with the flexibility required to manage variable workloads effectively. By leveraging its dynamic capabilities within the context of a well-defined supervision tree, applications can maintain robustness and reliability, even under dynamically changing conditions.

6.9 Using the Registry for Process Lookup

The Registry module in Elixir provides a scalable and efficient means for process lookup and management. This section elaborates on the functionality of Registry, its interaction with supervised processes, and practical implementations for various application requirements.

To initialize a Registry, it must be included as part of a supervision tree within your application. The following code demonstrates initiating a Registry under a supervisor:

```
def start_link(_) do
  children = [
    {Registry, keys: :unique, name: MyApp.Registry}
    # Other supervised children processes
  ]

  Supervisor.start_link(children, strategy: :one_for_one)
end
```

Here, the Registry is configured with a unique key attribute, ensuring that each process registered under a specific key is unique. The MyApp.Registry name identifies this registry instance.

Processes can then be registered in the Registry using the register/2 function from within a GenServer as follows:

```
def init(args) do
  {:ok, _} = Registry.register(MyApp.Registry, args[:name], [])
  {:ok, %{}}
```

```
end
```

In this example, args[:name] represents the key under which the process is registered. This key must be unique since the registry is configured with unique keys.

When a process needs to look up another process registered under a specific key, the lookup/2 function is utilized:

```
case Registry.lookup(MyApp.Registry, key) do
  [{pid, _value}] ->
    {:ok, pid}
  [] ->
    :error
end
```

The lookup/2 function returns a list of tuples, each containing the pid and the associated value. Since the registry has unique keys, the list is expected to have at most one entry.

Registry also supports match specifications, allowing complex queries. For example:

```
Registry.select(MyApp.Registry, [{{:"$1", :"$2", :_}, [{:==, :"$1", key}], [{{:"$1", :"$2
    "}}]}])
```

In this example, the match specification searches for entries where the key equals the value of key.

Updating process state in the Registry is possible with update_value/3. If a GenServer needs to update its state in the registry:

```
{:ok, _} = Registry.update_value(MyApp.Registry, key, fn value -> new_value end)
```

It is prudent to handle scenarios where a process may need to be unregistered. This can be achieved using the unregister/1 function as demonstrated:

```
Registry.unregister(MyApp.Registry, key)
```

This function removes the process associated with the given key from the registry. Additionally, when a registered process terminates, it is automatically deregistered.

One notable aspect of Registry is its ability to be partitioned for optimized performance across a multi-core system. The option :partitions configures the number of registry partitions, enhancing scalability:

```
{Registry, keys: :unique, name: MyApp.Registry, partitions: System.schedulers_online()
    }
```

By leveraging the System.schedulers_online/0 function, the registry is configured to use one partition per available CPU core.

Combining the registry with other OTP features, such as using DynamicSupervisor to initiate processes dynamically, extends its versatility. An example integration is illustrated below:

```
def start_task(name) do
  spec = %{
    id: name,
    start: {Task, :start_link, [fn -> task_work(name) end]},
    restart: :transient
  }
  DynamicSupervisor.start_child(MyApp.DynamicSupervisor, spec)
end

defp task_work(name) do
  Registry.register(MyApp.Registry, name, [])
  # Task implementation
end
```

Here, tasks are dynamically started under a dynamic supervisor and registered in the registry, allowing for easy lookup and management.

Incorporating these implementations optimizes process management and lookup, integral to designing robust and efficient Elixir applications leveraging OTP principles.

6.10 Building an OTP Application: A Hands-on Example

To illustrate the application of OTP principles in Elixir, we will build a simplified chat server application using GenServer and Supervisor. This example builds upon concepts introduced in previous sections, integrating them into a cohesive, functional system.

ChatServer will be a GenServer module responsible for handling chat room operations, including storing messages and managing users. A ChatSupervisor will manage instances of chat rooms, ensuring fault tolerance and recovery.

```
defmodule ChatServer do
  use GenServer

  # Client API

  def start_link(room_name) do
    GenServer.start_link(__MODULE__, %{}, name: via_tuple(room_name))
  end
```

```
  def send_message(room_name, message) do
    GenServer.cast(via_tuple(room_name), {:send_message, message})
  end

  def get_messages(room_name) do
    GenServer.call(via_tuple(room_name), :get_messages)
  end

  # Server Callbacks

  def init(_) do
    {:ok, %{messages: []}}
  end

  def handle_cast({:send_message, message}, state) do
    new_state = %{state | messages: [message | state.messages]}
    {:noreply, new_state}
  end

  def handle_call(:get_messages, _from, state) do
    {:reply, Enum.reverse(state.messages), state}
  end

  # Helper function to resolve process name via Registry
  defp via_tuple(room_name) do
    {:via, Registry, {ChatRegistry, room_name}}
  end
end
```

In this implementation:

- The start_link/1 function starts the GenServer process, associating it with a room name using a tuple via the Registry.
- The send_message/2 function casts a message to the server, which appends the message to the state.
- The get_messages/1 function calls the server to retrieve all stored messages.
- handle_cast/2 and handle_call/3 are callback functions that manage incoming cast and call requests, respectively.

Next, we define the ChatSupervisor to supervise ChatServer instances.

```
defmodule ChatSupervisor do
  use Supervisor

  def start_link(_) do
    Supervisor.start_link(__MODULE__, :ok, name: __MODULE__)
  end

  def init(:ok) do
    children = [
      {Registry, keys: :unique, name: ChatRegistry},
      %{
```

```
        id: ChatServer,
        start: {ChatServer, :start_link, []},
        type: :supervisor,
        strategy: :one_for_one
      }
    ]

    Supervisor.init(children, strategy: :one_for_one)
  end

  def start_chat_room(room_name) do
    Supervisor.start_child(__MODULE__,
      {ChatServer, [room_name]})
  end
end
```

In the ChatSupervisor module:

- start_link/1 starts the supervisor process.
- The init/1 function initializes the supervision tree, including a unique Registry for name resolution and the ChatServer.
- The start_chat_room/1 function dynamically starts a ChatServer child process.

Additionally, we create an application module to tie everything together:

```
defmodule ChatApp do
  use Application

  def start(_type, _args) do
    children = [
      ChatSupervisor
    ]

    opts = [strategy: :one_for_one, name: ChatApp.Supervisor]
    Supervisor.start_link(children, opts)
  end
end
```

In the ChatApp module:

- The start/2 callback starts the supervision tree with ChatSupervisor as its child.

To run our application, we add the following configuration to the mix.exs file:

```
defmodule ChatApp.MixProject do
  use Mix.Project

  def project do
    [
```

```
      app: :chat_app,
      version: "0.1.0",
      elixir: "~> 1.11",
      start_permanent: Mix.env() == :prod,
      deps: deps()
    ]
  end

  def application do
    [
      extra_applications: [:logger],
      mod: {ChatApp, []}
    ]
  end

  defp deps do
    []
  end
end
```

Once all these components are in place, we can run the application and interact with it:

```
$ mix run --no-halt

# In another terminal session:
iex> ChatSupervisor.start_chat_room("general")
{:ok, #PID<0.211.0>}

iex> ChatServer.send_message("general", "Hello World!")
:ok

iex> ChatServer.get_messages("general")
["Hello World!"]
```

This example demonstrates the construction of a basic yet functional OTP application. It integrates GenServer for process management and Supervisor for process supervision, ensuring fault tolerance and scalability within the application architecture. The use of the Registry facilitates dynamic process identification and communication within the system.

Chapter 7

Mix and Project Management

This chapter explores Mix, Elixir's build tool, and project management. It demonstrates creating new projects, understanding project structure, and managing dependencies. The chapter covers compiling and running code, using Mix tasks, handling environments and configurations, and generating documentation. Additionally, it addresses testing with Mix, publishing packages, and deploying Elixir applications, providing comprehensive guidance for managing Elixir projects efficiently. Certainly! Here is the corrected LaTeX section addressing the reported error and ensuring the proper formatting guidelines:

"'latex

7.1 Introduction to Mix

Mix is the build tool that accompanies the Elixir language, permitting the development, management, and maintenance of projects in a streamlined manner. Mix offers a variety of features, including project creation, compilation, dependency management, environment-specific configuration, testing, and more. This section aims to provide a detailed understanding of Mix's capabilities and its significance in managing Elixir projects.

Core Features of Mix

Mix is designed to simplify numerous aspects of project management in Elixir. Core capabilities include:

- **Project Creation**: Mix generates new projects with standard directory structures and predefined configurations.
- **Dependency Management**: Mix handles the fetching, updating, and compiling of project dependencies.
- **Compilation and Build**: Mix compiles the project's source code and assets, ensuring that the build process is seamless and efficient.
- **Task Automation**: Mix provides a robust framework for defining and running custom tasks, enhancing automation within the development workflow.
- **Environment Management**: Mix supports different configurations for various environments (e.g., development, test, and production) facilitating diverse use cases.
- **Testing and Documentation**: Mix integrates testing frameworks and documentation tools, promoting best practices in software development.

Installation and Setup

Mix is bundled with Elixir, so no additional installation steps are necessary beyond setting up Elixir itself. Assuming Elixir is correctly installed, invoking Mix can be done via the terminal with the following command:

```
$ mix
```

Executing this command will display a list of available Mix tasks:

```
mix                  # Displays all available tasks
mix app.start          # Starts all registered apps
mix compile            # Compiles source files
mix deps.get           # Fetches dependencies
mix test              # Runs tests
...
```

Creating a New Project

To create a new Elixir project, Mix provides the `mix new` command followed by the name of the project. For instance, to create a project named `my_project`, execute:

```
$ mix new my_project
```

This command generates a new directory named my_project with a predefined structure, including subdirectories for configuration files, source code, tests, dependencies, and more. The layout will resemble the following:

```
my_project/
    config/
        config.exs
    lib/
        my_project.ex
    test/
        my_project_test.exs
    mix.exs
    README.md
    .gitignore
```

Understanding Mix Project Structure

Each generated project will contain several important files and directories:

- mix.exs: Main configuration file located at the root directory. It defines project metadata such as name, version, dependencies, and build specific settings.
- config/: Contains configuration files. The config.exs file within this directory is utilized for standard environment configurations.
- lib/: Main source code directory. It includes the primary module for the application and other source files.
- test/: This directory comprises test files. Mix generates it with a sample test to ensure the test framework is operational.
- README.md: A Markdown file typically containing an overview of the project, setup instructions, and other relevant documentation.
- .gitignore: A template Gitignore file tailored for Elixir projects to exclude build artifacts and unnecessary files from version control.

Defining and Managing Dependencies

Dependencies are essential for almost every non-trivial Elixir project. Mix simplifies dependency management through the mix.exs file. Dependencies are specified using the :deps key within the project function:

```
defp deps do
  [
    {:plug_cowboy, "~> 2.5"}
  ]
end
```

In this example, the plug_cowboy library is added as a dependency. The ~2.5 denotes that versions up to, but not including, 3.0 are acceptable.

Once dependencies are defined, they can be fetched and compiled using:

```
$ mix deps.get
$ mix deps.compile
```

This will download and compile all specified dependencies, making them available to the project.

Understanding these foundational aspects of Mix provides a solid foundation for leveraging its full capabilities in project management. Subsequent sections will delve deeper into each functionality, illustrating how to maximize the effectiveness of Mix in real-world Elixir development.

7.2 Creating a New Project

When starting a new Elixir project, the primary tool you'll interact with is Mix, which serves as the build tool and package manager for Elixir. This tool automates many common tasks and streamlines the entire workflow, making the process of creating, compiling, and managing projects efficient.

To create a new Elixir project, you will use the mix new command followed by the name of the project. The syntax for this command is straightforward:

```
$ mix new project_name
```

For instance, to create a project named my_app, you would run:

```
$ mix new my_app
```

Upon executing this command, Mix generates a new directory named my_app and populates it with a predefined project structure. This foundational structure includes essential files and directories that facilitate application development and organization.

The structure of a new Elixir project is as follows:

```
my_app/
|-- _build/
|-- config/
|   '-- config.exs
|-- lib/
|   '-- my_app.ex
|-- test/
|   |-- my_app_test.exs
|   '-- test_helper.exs
|-- mix.exs
|-- README.md
|-- .gitignore
```

Project Structure and Files

- _build/: This directory contains compiled files and project-specific build artifacts. It is automatically generated during compilation and used by Mix to manage various environments such as dev, test, and prod.

- config/: This directory houses configuration files. The primary configuration file is config.exs, which contains configuration settings for the application and its dependencies. Custom environment configurations can be added within this directory.

- lib/: The lib directory is where the primary source code of your application resides. The file my_app.ex is generated by default and typically contains the main module of the application.

- test/: This directory includes test files. my_app_test.exs is the default test file for the main module, and test_helper.exs sets up the test environment. Tests are structured using the ExUnit framework, which is integrated into Elixir.

- mix.exs: This file is the Mix project file and serves as the entry point for defining various properties of the project, such as dependencies, version, and application information. The contents of a default mix.exs file look like this:

```
defmodule MyApp.MixProject do
  use Mix.Project

  def project do
    [
      app: :my_app,
      version: "0.1.0",
      elixir: "~> 1.10",
      start_permanent: Mix.env() == :prod,
      deps: deps()
    ]
  end
```

```
  def application do
    [
      extra_applications: [:logger]
    ]
  end

  defp deps do
    []
  end
end
```

In this file, app/0 defines the name of the application, version/0 specifies the version, elixir/0 indicates the Elixir version compatibility, start_-permanent/0 ensures the application runs in permanent mode in production, and deps/0 lists the project dependencies. The application/0 function returns a keyword list of applications to start.

- README.md: A markdown file where you can include information about the project, its purpose, usage instructions, and any other relevant details.

- .gitignore: This file specifies intentionally untracked files to ignore in the Git repository. By default, it includes files and directories such as _build, deps, and other typical entries that should not be committed to version control.

Running the Project

After creating the project, navigate into the project directory:

```
$ cd my_app
```

You can then compile and run the project using Mix commands. To compile the project, use:

```
$ mix compile
```

This command compiles all the code in the project. Any errors or warnings are displayed to help ensure that your code is functioning correctly. If the compilation succeeds, you can run the project by starting an IEx session with the project loaded:

```
$ iex -S mix
```

The command above launches an interactive Elixir shell with the project's environment loaded, allowing you to test and debug your application interactively.

Mix also provides functionality for running tests. The following command executes all tests in the project:

```
$ mix test
```

Test results and potential failed test cases are displayed, offering immediate feedback on the stability and correctness of the code.

Customizing Project Creation

Mix allows the use of options to customize the creation of a new project. For example, you can create a supervisor tree instead of a simple module by using the –sup option:

```
$ mix new my_app --sup
```

This generates a project with a supervision tree, which includes additional files and dependencies necessary for managing application processes effectively. The resultant project structure adds an application.ex file in the lib directory for setting up the supervision tree.

Likewise, other options such as –module, –app, and -v provide further customization for module names, application names, and verbosity of outputs.

Mix empowers developers to create new projects with ease, ensuring a consistent and organized structure conducive to maintaining and scaling applications. By utilizing Mix's powerful project creation capabilities, developers can focus more on coding and less on project setup intricacies.

7.3 Project Structure and Files

The structural organization of an Elixir project is pivotal for maintaining readability, scalability, and ease of collaboration. When you create a new project using Mix, a typical directory layout is automatically generated. Understanding this layout is essential for effective project management and development.

Upon creating a new Mix project using:

```
$ mix new project_name
```

the following directory structure is generated:

```
project_name/
|-- _build/
```

```
|-- config/
|   |-- config.exs
|-- lib/
|   |-- project_name.ex
|   |-- project_name/
|-- test/
|   |-- project_name_test.exs
|   |-- test_helper.exs
|-- mix.exs
|-- README.md
```

Each directory and file plays a specific role in the project's architecture:

- _build/ **Directory:** This is where Mix stores the build artifacts, such as compiled bytecode. Typically, developers do not need to manually manipulate or examine files within this directory. It includes different subdirectories for each environment, such as dev, test, and prod.

- config/ **Directory:** Configuration files for the project are housed here. The primary file is config.exs, which provides a centralized place to manage various configuration settings. This file might include environment-specific settings through conditional configuration blocks. It is common to have additional environment-specific configuration files such as dev.exs, test.exs, and prod.exs for development, testing, and production environments, respectively.

The config.exs might look like this:

```
use Mix.Config

config :project_name,
  key: "value"
```

- lib/ **Directory:** The main directory for your application's source code. It generally contains:

- project_name.ex**:** Defines the main module of your application. It might include the start/2 function, which kicks off the supervision tree for your application.

- project_name/ **Directory:** A namespace folder that prevents module name collisions and aids in structuring larger applications. As your project grows, additional directories and modules can be added here in a well-organized manner.

```
defmodule ProjectName do
  use Application

  def start(_type, _args) do
    children = [
      # Define workers and child supervisors to be supervised
    ]

    opts = [strategy: :one_for_one, name: ProjectName.Supervisor]
    Supervisor.start_link(children, opts)
  end
end
```

- test/ **Directory:** Contains the test files for your application. It generally includes:
- project_name_test.exs**:** The primary test file generated by Mix. It uses the ExUnit framework to define and run tests.
- test_helper.exs**:** A helper file executed before your tests run, setting up the test environment.

An example of a basic test setup might look like:

```
defmodule ProjectNameTest do
  use ExUnit.Case
  doctest ProjectName

  test "the truth" do
    assert 1 + 1 == 2
  end
end
```

- mix.exs **File:** This is the main configuration file for your Mix project, containing metadata about the project, its dependencies, and environment-specific settings. The mix.exs file typically includes various functions such as project/0, application/0, and deps/0. Each of these functions specifies essential elements such as the project's version, Elixir version compatibility, application start behavior, and dependency list.

Here is a typical example of a mix.exs file:

```
defmodule ProjectName.MixProject do
  use Mix.Project

  def project do
    [
      app: :project_name,
      version: "0.1.0",
```

```
      elixir: "~> 1.11",
      start_permanent: Mix.env() == :prod,
      deps: deps()
    ]
  end

  def application do
    [
      extra_applications: [:logger]
    ]
  end

  defp deps do
    [
      {:dependency_name, "~> 1.0.0"}
    ]
  end
end
```

- README.md **File:** Provides an introductory manual and often includes instructions on setting up and using the project, contributing guidelines, and other relevant documentation. This markdown file serves as a rich text that offers documentation and is frequently the first point of reference for users and contributors.

The generated structure and files offer a robust foundation for developing Elixir applications. It not only provides a clear and organized starting point but also supports the essential practices of modular design, separation of concerns, and maintainability.

7.4 Managing Dependencies

Dependencies are an integral part of any modern software project, enhancing functionality by allowing you to leverage external libraries and tools. In Elixir projects, dependencies are managed through Mix. This section provides a detailed explanation on how to manage dependencies using Mix, covering the declaration, fetching, updating, and removing of dependencies.

Dependencies in Mix projects are declared in the mix.exs file. This file contains the project configuration, including a deps function that returns a list of tuples, each representing a dependency. The general syntax for specifying a dependency is as follows:

```
defp deps do
  [
    {:dep_from_hexpm, "~> 0.3.0"},
```

```
    {:some_git_repo, git: "https://github.com/elixir-lang/my_dep.git", tag: "0.1.0"}
  ]
end
```

The first element of each tuple is the name of the dependency. The second element can be a version string or a keyword list that specifies additional options such as the Git repository URL and the tag, branch, or commit to use.

To fetch and install the declared dependencies, run the following command:

```
mix deps.get
```

This command reads the mix.exs file, resolves the dependencies, and downloads them to the deps directory. Mix also generates a mix.lock file that records the exact versions of the installed dependencies, ensuring that the same dependency versions are used across different environments and systems.

If you need to update the dependencies to their latest versions as specified in the version requirements, use:

```
mix deps.update --all
```

This command updates all dependencies listed in the deps function to the latest versions that match the specified version constraints. If you want to update a specific dependency, you can specify its name, for example:

```
mix deps.update dep_from_hexpm
```

To remove a dependency, simply delete its entry from the deps function in mix.exs, and then run:

```
mix deps.clean --unused
```

This command removes any dependencies that are no longer required by the project.

Additionally, Mix provides a way to specify optional dependencies that can be included only in certain environments. This is achieved using environment-specific configuration. For example, you may want to include a dependency only in the :test environment:

```
defp deps do
  [
    {:ex_unit, "~> 1.11", only: :test}
  ]
```

```
end
```

In this case, the ex_unit dependency will only be available when running tests, reducing overhead in other environments.

Mix also supports umbrella projects, where multiple related applications are managed within a single repository. Dependencies in umbrella projects can be split between the root project and individual child applications. Dependencies shared across child applications should be declared in the root mix.exs, while specific dependencies can be defined in each child application's mix.exs. For example, a root mix.exs might look like this:

```
defp deps do
  [
    {:ecto, "~> 3.5"},
    {:phoenix, "~> 1.5"}
  ]
end
```

And the child application's mix.exs:

```
defp deps do
  [
    {:ex_machina, "~> 2.3"}
  ]
end
```

When working within an umbrella project, dependencies are fetched and managed in a unified manner, ensuring consistent versions and reducing duplication.

Finally, Elixir's dependency management supports overriding default dependency behaviors, allowing fine-tuned control over content loading and compilation. For example, you might disable the runtime option for a library that is only needed at compile time:

```
defp deps do
  [
    {:some_dep, "~> 0.1", runtime: false}
  ]
end
```

Through these methods, Mix provides comprehensive and flexible dependency management tailored to the needs of Elixir projects at various scales and complexities.

7.5 Compiling and Running Code

Compiling and running code are fundamental operations in any Elixir project, facilitated by the Mix build tool. This section outlines the procedures and commands necessary for efficient compilation and execution of Elixir applications.

The mix compile command is utilized to compile the source code of an Elixir project. This command reads all the source files located in the lib directory, along with any dependency files, and compiles them into .beam files. The .beam files are the compiled versions of the Elixir files and are stored in the _build directory.

```
$ mix compile
```

Executing mix compile will produce output indicating the progress and any warnings or errors encountered during compilation. The command is designed to compile only the files that have changed since the last compilation, enhancing efficiency. To force a complete recompilation of all files, use the –force option:

```
$ mix compile --force
```

If there are no compilation issues, the terminal will output a message such as:

```
Compiled lib/my_app.ex
Generated my_app app
```

Moreover, Mix offers a convenient approach for running the compiled code. The primary mechanism is the mix run command which can be employed with or without arguments to execute specific files or initiate a script.

To execute an Elixir script directly:

```
$ mix run path/to/script.exs
```

When running a complete application, especially one with an entry point defined in mix.exs, simply use:

```
$ mix run --no-halt
```

The –no-halt flag ensures the application keeps running, essential for applications expecting continuous operations, such as web servers or background processing services.

An efficient workflow often involves automatically compiling the project when running scripts. This can be achieved by combining the mix run command with modules or functions directly. Here is an example of running a module's function:

```
$ mix run -e 'MyApp.Module.function()'
```

The -e flag allows the execution of specific expressions or function calls. This method is particularly useful for running short-lived scripts or exploring functions during development.

The following is a simple Elixir module with a function to illustrate this process. Consider the file lib/my_app/module.ex:

```
defmodule MyApp.Module do
  def function do
    IO.puts "Hello, World!"
  end
end
```

Running the above function using mix run will yield:

```
Hello, World!
```

Compiling and running code in different environments can be crucial due to varying configurations. Mix supports different environments, typically :dev, :test, and :prod, managed via the MIX_ENV environment variable. By default, Mix operates in the :dev environment. Explicitly setting the environment is done as follows:

```
$ MIX_ENV=prod mix compile
```

This command compiles the codebase in production mode, leveraging configurations specified for the prod environment which might differ from development settings. Similarly, running an application in a specified environment, such as production, is performed by:

```
$ MIX_ENV=prod mix run --no-halt
```

By understanding the nuances of compiling and running Elixir code using Mix, developers can effectively manage their workflow, ensuring their projects compile optimally and execute as expected in various environments.

7.6 Using Mix Tasks

Mix tasks are an integral component of Elixir's build and project management tool, Mix. They simplify and automate various workflows involved in the development and maintenance of Elixir projects. This section delves into the utilization of Mix tasks, covering both the built-in tasks and the creation of custom tasks.

Mix provides numerous built-in tasks that facilitate common project operations such as compiling code, running tests, and managing dependencies. To list all available Mix tasks for a project, the following command is used:

```
mix help
```

Executing this command displays a comprehensive list of tasks tailored to the current project's context. Each task can be invoked by running mix <task_name>. For instance, to compile a project, the command below is executed:

```
mix compile
```

This command compiles source files in the lib directory, generating bytecode in the _build directory. Compilation is a prerequisite for running an application and for performing other tasks that depend on compiled code.

Another frequently used task is mix test, which runs the tests defined in the test directory. By running:

```
mix test
```

Developers can ensure their code behaves as expected. Mix captures and displays the outcome of each test, including any errors or failures encountered.

Mix tasks are powerful due to their ability to be parameterized, allowing them to adapt to different scenarios. For example, the mix compile task can include additional flags to control its behavior. The following example recompiles only the changed files:

```
mix compile --force
```

Built-in Mix tasks greatly enhance development efficiency; however, there are situations that necessitate custom tasks tailored to specific project needs. Creating a custom Mix task involves several steps, starting with defining the task module, which must reside in the lib/mix/-tasks directory. A custom task is identified by the Mix.Task behaviour and its corresponding module name must be prefixed with Mix.Tasks.

Consider the following example, which creates a simple Mix task called hello:

```
# File: lib/mix/tasks/hello.ex
defmodule Mix.Tasks.Hello do
  use Mix.Task

  @shortdoc "Prints Hello, World!"
  def run(_) do
    Mix.shell().info("Hello, World!")
  end
end
```

In the example above, the task is defined within the Mix.Tasks.Hello module. The use Mix.Task line is mandatory as it provides the necessary behaviour for the module to be recognized as a Mix task. The @shortdoc module attribute provides a brief description of the task, which will appear in the task list when mix help is run. The run function encompasses the task's functionality, and the argument _ denotes that the task does not require any specific input parameters.

To execute the newly created task, the following command is used:

```
mix hello
```

Upon execution, the task prints Hello, World! to the console, illustrating how straightforward it is to augment Mix with custom tasks.

Custom tasks can also accept command-line arguments for enhanced flexibility. By parsing arguments within the run function, tasks can exhibit dynamic behavior based on input parameters. Consider extending the previous example to greet a specific user:

```
# File: lib/mix/tasks/greet.ex
defmodule Mix.Tasks.Greet do
  use Mix.Task

  @shortdoc "Greets a user"
  def run(args) do
    name = parse_args(args)
    Mix.shell().info("Hello, #{name}!")
  end

  defp parse_args([name | _]), do: name
  defp parse_args(_), do: "World"
end
```

In this implementation, the run function calls parse_args, a helper function that extracts the user's name from the command-line arguments. If no name is provided, it defaults to "World". To execute the task with an argument:

```
mix greet Alice
```

The task now prints Hello, Alice!, adjusting the output based on the provided argument.

Mix tasks can also utilize the OptionParser module to handle more complex argument structures, including flags and switches. This module facilitates the declaration and parsing of expected parameters, enhancing the task's robustness and usability. The following example demonstrates parsing named options:

```
# File: lib/mix/tasks/greet.ex
defmodule Mix.Tasks.Greet do
  use Mix.Task

  @shortdoc "Greets a user"
  def run(args) do
    {opts, _, _} = OptionParser.parse(args, switches: [loud: :boolean])
    name = parse_args(args)
    greeting = if opts[:loud], do: String.upcase("Hello, #{name}!"), else: "Hello, #{
        name}!"
    Mix.shell().info(greeting)
  end

  defp parse_args([name | _]), do: name
  defp parse_args(_), do: "World"
end
```

In this version, the task supports a –loud flag, which, when provided, converts the greeting to uppercase. The OptionParser module is employed to declare and parse the flag. The task now handles more complex input and adjusts its behavior accordingly.

The ability to create custom Mix tasks empowers developers to streamline development processes, automate repetitive tasks, and integrate bespoke workflows into their projects. These tasks can be as simple or as complex as necessary, providing a robust framework for enhancing productivity in Elixir projects.

7.7 Environment and Configuration Management

Elixir provides robust support for managing different environments and configurations in applications. This section delves into how developers can manage configurations for different environments (e.g., development, test, and production), leveraging Mix for environment-specific settings, and the appropriate methods for configuring Elixir applications.

Configurations in Elixir are typically managed using configuration files located in the config directory of your project. This directory is part of the standard project structure created by Mix and usually contains config.exs, dev.exs, test.exs, and prod.exs files. Each of these files corresponds to specific environments and holds environment-specific settings.

```
config/
  config.exs # Shared configurations
  dev.exs # Configuration for the development environment
  test.exs # Configuration for the test environment
  prod.exs # Configuration for the production environment
```

The config.exs file contains the shared configuration settings applicable across all environments. This file is automatically loaded before any environment-specific configuration files.

```
use Mix.Config

config :my_app, key: :value

import_config "#{Mix.env}.exs"
```

In the above snippet, Mix.env dynamically determines the current Mix environment, allowing the corresponding dev.exs, test.exs, or prod.exs to be imported. Mix environments can be changed using the MIX_ENV environment variable when running Mix tasks. For instance, to run the tests in the test environment, use:

```
$ MIX_ENV=test mix test
```

Elixir's Mix.Config module, employed in config.exs, ensures that configurations are easy to read and maintain. Below is a brief explanation of how to structure and manage different environment configurations.

```
use Mix.Config

config :my_app, MyApp.Repo,
```

```
  username: "postgres",
  password: "postgres",
  database: "my_app_dev",
  hostname: "localhost",
  pool_size: 10
```

In dev.exs, the database settings for the development environment are specified, such as the username, password, and database name. Similar configurations can be set in test.exs and prod.exs, adjusted accordingly to fit those environments.

Managing Configuration for Different Environments

Environment-specific configurations are crucial, especially when working with sensitive data like database credentials, secret keys, and API tokens. It is advisable to load such secrets from the system environment variables to avoid hardcoding them in configuration files. The System.get_env/1 function can be used for this purpose.

```
use Mix.Config

config :my_app, MyApp.Repo,
  username: System.get_env("DB_USERNAME"),
  password: System.get_env("DB_PASSWORD"),
  database: System.get_env("DB_NAME"),
  hostname: "localhost",
  pool_size: 15,
  ssl: true
```

The ssl: true setting illustrates configuring the production environment with SSL enabled for enhanced security. It's best practice to ensure that sensitive information is not hardcoded but retrieved securely at runtime.

Furthermore, the config/releases.exs file comes into play when dealing with Elixir releases using tools like Distillery or Mix Releases. This file allows runtime configuration of settings without requiring recompilation, promoting flexibility in production environments.

```
import Config

config :my_app, MyApp.Repo,
  username: System.fetch_env!("DB_USERNAME"),
  password: System.fetch_env!("DB_PASSWORD"),
  database: System.fetch_env!("DB_NAME"),
  hostname: System.fetch_env!("DB_HOSTNAME"),
  pool_size: System.fetch_env!("POOL_SIZE") |> String.to_integer()
```

The System.fetch_env!/1 function raises an error if the environment variable is missing, thus providing a safeguard ensuring all required configurations are present.

Another critical consideration is using config/runtime.exs to manage configurations that need to be evaluated at runtime. The benefit of runtime.exs is that it is only executed when the system starts, making it ideal for configurations dependent on runtime system state.

```
import Config

if config_env() == :prod do
  config :my_app, MyApp.Repo,
    username: System.fetch_env!("DB_USERNAME"),
    password: System.fetch_env!("DB_PASSWORD"),
    database: System.fetch_env!("DB_NAME"),
    hostname: System.fetch_env!("DB_HOSTNAME"),
    pool_size: String.to_integer(System.fetch_env!("POOL_SIZE"))
end
```

In this example, the configuration is dynamically adjusted based on the environment obtained at runtime, specifically tuned for the production environment.

Managing environment and configuration settings efficiently ensures that an Elixir application remains predictable, secure, and adaptable across various stages of its lifecycle. Employing system environment variables and leveraging runtime configuration files like runtime.exs play a pivotal role in maintaining operational excellence and adherence to best practices.

7.8 Using Mix for Documentation

Mix provides extensive support for generating project documentation, leveraging the capabilities of ExDoc—a documentation generation tool specifically built for Elixir projects. To facilitate this, Mix integrates various tasks that automate the creation and management of documentation, ensuring it is an integral component of the development lifecycle.

To begin generating documentation, first ensure the ex_doc dependency is included in your project's dependencies. This is typically specified in the mix.exs file as follows:

```
defp deps do
  [
    {:ex_doc, "~> 0.24", only: :dev, runtime: false}
  ]
end
```

After adding the dependency, fetch and compile the new dependency by running:

```
$ mix deps.get
$ mix deps.compile
```

Once the dependency is in place, Mix can generate the documentation using the mix docs task. This task compiles the project's source code, extracts the documentation from module attributes and function annotations, and generates HTML files which can be easily viewed in a web browser.

To generate the documentation, execute:

```
$ mix docs
```

By default, the generated documentation is placed in the doc directory within the project's root. You can open the index.html file in a web browser to access the documentation and verify its contents.

Proper documentation in Elixir follows specific conventions:

- **Module Documentation**: The documentation for a module is provided via the @moduledoc attribute. This attribute is typically placed at the beginning of the module and should describe the purpose, functionality, and usage of the module.
- **Function Documentation**: Individual functions within a module are documented using the @doc attribute. This attribute is placed immediately before the function definition and should explain the function's purpose, parameters, and return values. Examples can be included within the @doc attribute to illustrate usage.

Consider an illustrative example module with proper documentation annotations:

```
defmodule ExampleModule do
  @moduledoc """
  This module provides example functions to demonstrate documentation practices.
  """

  @doc """
  Adds two numbers.

  ## Parameters:

    - x: The first number.
    - y: The second number.

  ## Examples:

      iex> ExampleModule.add(1, 2)
      3
```

```
  """
  def add(x, y) do
    x + y
  end

  @doc """
  Multiplies two numbers.

  ## Parameters:

    - a: The first number.
    - b: The second number.

  ## Examples:

      iex> ExampleModule.multiply(2, 3)
      6

  """
  def multiply(a, b) do
    a * b
  end
end
```

In the example above, the @moduledoc attribute provides an overview of the ExampleModule, while the @doc attributes for the add and multiply functions specify their purposes, parameters, and provide example usages.

Mix and ExDoc support generating additional types of documentation, such as:

- **Types and Specifications**: Documenting type specifications using @spec annotations to specify the expected types of arguments and return values. These annotations improve code clarity and provide additional context for users of the functions.
- **Callbacks**: Properly documenting callback functions for behaviours to define expected implementations for modules adhering to a specific behaviour.

An advanced configuration of the documentation process can be accomplished by customizing the mix.exs file. For instance, one can specify different options for the :ex_doc dependency to alter the output directory, adjust formatting, and include additional documentation assets.

Here is an example customization in the mix.exs:

```
def project do
  [
```

```
    app: :example,
    version: "0.1.0",
    elixir: "~> 1.11",
    start_permanent: Mix.env() == :prod,
    deps: deps(),
    docs: [
      main: "readme",
      extras: ["README.md"],
      output: "custom_docs"
    ]
  ]
end
```

In this case, the main option designates README.md as the main page of the documentation, while the extras option includes additional markdown files. The output option specifies a custom output directory for the generated documentation.

Mix also provides utilities for ensuring documentation is kept up-to-date. The mix hex.docs commands are particularly useful for publishing documentation to HexDocs, the online documentation resource for Hex packages. This process involves creating a Hex account, configuring authentication, and executing the following task:

```
$ mix hex.docs.publish
```

Using Mix for documentation ensures comprehensiveness and consistency across modules and functions. It integrates seamlessly with the development workflow, promoting best practices and enhancing the utility and readability of the codebase.

7.9 Running Tests with Mix

Testing is integral to software development, ensuring correctness and reliability in code. Mix, Elixir's build tool, offers robust support for testing through the mix test task.

```
$ mix test
```

Executing mix test in the terminal runs all the tests defined in the project. Mix conventionally looks for tests within the test directory. The output categorizes test results, displaying the number of passed, failed, and skipped tests, along with any error messages and stack traces.

```
.

Finished in 0.05 seconds
1 test, 0 failures
```

To organize tests, Elixir employs the ExUnit framework, which is built into the standard library. Tests are defined in modules, and each test case is a function prefixed with test. By convention, test module names correspond to the module being tested, appended with Test.

```
defmodule CalculatorTest do
  use ExUnit.Case

  test "addition of two numbers" do
    assert Calculator.add(1, 2) == 3
  end
end
```

In this instance, the test asserts that the add function of the Calculator module returns 3 when provided with the arguments 1 and 2. Tests utilize the assert macro to verify expected outcomes.

To delve deeper, ExUnit supports various macros to handle different assertions:

- assert – Verifies that an expression evaluates to true.
- refute – Confirms that an expression evaluates to false.
- assert_raise – Checks for raised exceptions.

```
defmodule MyTest do
  use ExUnit.Case

  test "string contains substring" do
    assert String.contains?("hello world", "world")
  end

  test "list is empty" do
    refute Enum.empty?([1, 2, 3])
  end

  test "raises a function clause error" do
    assert_raise FunctionClauseError, fn ->
      String.upcase(:atom)
    end
  end
end
```

For more intricate tests, setup and teardown functionality is necessary. This is managed through the setup and on_exit callbacks.

```
defmodule ComplexTest do
  use ExUnit.Case

  setup do
    {:ok, value: 42}
  end
```

```
  test "value is accessible", context do
    assert context[:value] == 42
  end

  on_exit fn ->
    IO.puts("Test case completed")
  end
end
```

Here, the setup callback prepares the test environment, returning a map of key-value pairs. Each test can access these pairs through the context parameter. The on_exit callback ensures that specified code runs after each test, facilitating cleanup tasks.

More comprehensive testing strategies involve test coverage and property-based testing. Mix integrates well with ex_coveralls for test coverage reporting.

```
$ mix deps.get ex_coveralls
```

Add ex_coveralls to the mix.exs dependencies:

```
defp deps do
  [
    {:ex\_coveralls, "~> 0.11", only: :test}
  ]
end
```

To generate coverage reports:

```
$ mix coveralls.html
```

This command outputs a detailed HTML report depicting which parts of the codebase are covered by tests.

For property-based testing, akin to generative testing, use the PropCheck library, providing a way to run tests with a wide range of arbitrary inputs, thereby verifying the robustness of code under various scenarios.

```
$ mix deps.get propcheck
```

Include PropCheck in mix.exs:

```
defp deps do
  [
    {:propcheck, "~> 1.4", only: :test}
  ]
end
```

Leveraging the properties in test modules provides automated checks for expected behaviors:

```
defmodule ListPropertiesTest do
  use ExUnit.Case
  use PropCheck

  property "reverse reverses a list correctly" do
    forall list <- list(integer()) do
      assert Enum.reverse(Enum.reverse(list)) == list
    end
  end
end
```

Tests can also be filtered using tags for selective execution. This is highly beneficial in large projects:

```
defmodule AliasedTest do
  use ExUnit.Case, async: true

  @tag :focus
  test "only run focused tests" do
    assert 1 + 1 == 2
  end
end
```

Run focused tests using:

```
$ mix test --only focus
```

Comprehensive testing within Mix ensures robust software quality, augmenting development practices across multiple complexity levels.

7.10 Publishing and Managing Packages

Publishing and managing packages in Elixir is facilitated through Hex, the package manager for the Erlang ecosystem. This section elaborates on the processes involved in creating, publishing, and maintaining packages using Mix and Hex. We begin by setting up prerequisites and walk through the steps required to publish a new package. Following this, we delve into managing the package lifecycle, including versioning and updating packages.

Prerequisites: Before publishing a package, ensure that you have the latest version of Elixir and Hex installed. Verify the installation using the following commands:

```
elixir --version
mix hex.info
```

Setting Up a New Package: Creating a new package starts with the

Mix tool. First, generate a new project if not already created:

```
mix new my_new_package
cd my_new_package
```

Next, we'll configure mix.exs, the file where various project configuration settings are specified. Open mix.exs and ensure it includes necessary metadata.

```
defmodule MyNewPackage.MixProject do
  use Mix.Project

  def project do
    [
      app: :my_new_package,
      version: "0.1.0",
      elixir: "~> 1.11",
      start_permanent: Mix.env() == :prod,
      deps: deps(),
      description: "A concise description of the package",
      package: package(),
      name: "my_new_package",
      source_url: "https://github.com/username/my_new_package"
    ]
  end

  defp package do
    [
      licenses: ["MIT"],
      links: %{"GitHub" => "https://github.com/username/my_new_package"},
      files: ~w(lib mix.exs README.md LICENSE CHANGELOG.md)
    ]
  end

  def application do
    [
      extra_applications: [:logger]
    ]
  end

  defp deps do
    []
  end
end
```

Key fields to note:

* name - The package name in lowercase and underscore format. * version - The initial version following semantic versioning. * description - A brief description of the package. * package - Metadata necessary for Hex, including license, links for documentation, and files to include.

Documentation and Tests: Ensure you have comprehensive documentation and tests before releasing the package. Elixir's ExDoc can be used to generate HTML documentation.

Add ex_doc to your dependencies in mix.exs:

```
defp deps do
  [
    {:ex_doc, "~> 0.22", only: :dev, runtime: false}
  ]
end
```

Run the following command to generate the documentation:

```
mix docs
```

Testing your package can be performed using:

```
mix test
```

Publishing the Package: Before the initial release, authenticate with Hex:

```
mix hex.user register
```

Follow the prompts to create your Hex account if you don't have one. Once registered, publish the package:

```
mix hex.publish
```

This command will prompt for confirmation and display the package details to be published. Verify the information and confirm to complete the publish process.

Versioning and Updating Packages: Follow semantic versioning for managing your package versions:

* Increment the major version for incompatible API changes. * Increment the minor version for added functionality in a backwards-compatible manner. * Increment the patch version for backwards-compatible bug fixes.

Make necessary updates to the code, and increment the version in mix.exs. To publish an updated version, use:

```
mix hex.publish
```

Managing Package Dependencies: To specify dependencies for your package, add the required libraries in the deps function in mix.exs. For instance:

```
defp deps do
  [
    {:ecto, "~> 3.6"},
    {:phoenix, "~> 1.5"}
  ]
end
```

Use mix deps.get to fetch the dependencies:

```
mix deps.get
```

Retiring a Package: If a package becomes obsolete, you may retire it to indicate that it should no longer be used. Retirement is done with:

```
mix hex.retire package_name version
```

Specify a reason for retirement, such as renamed, deprecated, or security, and provide an optional message for users.

Engaging in package management with clear documentation and diligent versioning practices ensures robustness and wide usability of your Elixir packages.

7.11 Deploying Elixir Applications

Deploying an Elixir application is a critical step in the development process, transforming code from a development environment to a production-ready state. This section details the process of preparing and deploying Elixir applications, employing Mix tools and other essential utilities to ensure reliable and efficient deployment.

Elixir applications are often deployed as releases, which are self-contained executables that include the Erlang virtual machine (VM) and all required dependencies. Releases ensure application portability and simplify the deployment process since all necessary components are bundled together.

```
mix release
```

Executing mix release compiles the project and assembles a release in the _build/prod/rel directory. The command considers settings from the config/prod.exs file, ensuring that production-specific configurations are applied.

```
_build/
  prod/
    rel/
      my_app/
        bin/
        erts-XX.XX/
        lib/
        releases/
        tmp/
```

The release directory contains the following subdirectories:

- bin: Contains scripts to start, stop, and manage the release.
- erts-XX.XX: Includes the Erlang runtime components.
- lib: Houses compiled bytecode and dependencies.
- releases: Stores metadata about the release.
- tmp: Temporary files and sockets for the release.

Mix uses distillery or elixir_release behind the scenes to create releases. These tools offer numerous configuration options to tailor the release process. You can fine-tune the release settings in the rel/config.exs file.

```
# rel/config.exs
use Mix.Releases.Config

environment :prod do
  set(include_erts: true)
  set(include_src: false)
  set(cookie: :"\$MY_COOKIE")
end

release :my_app do
  set(version: current_version(:my_app))
  set(applications: [
    :runtime_tools
  ])
end
```

The configuration enables the use of different environments (:prod, :dev, etc.), specifying critical settings like include_erts, include_src, and the cookie for distributed nodes.

After creating a release, you can deploy it to the target server. Deployments often involve transferring the release to a server, extracting it, and starting the application. Commonly used tools include SSH and deployment automation services such as Ansible or Chef.

```
scp _build/prod/rel/my_app/releases/0.1.0/my_app.tar.gz user@server:/path/to
    /deploy
ssh user@server
cd /path/to/deploy
tar -xzvf my_app.tar.gz
```

After extracting the release, start the application using the provided scripts:

```
cd /path/to/deploy/my_app
bin/my_app start
```

You can manage the release using various commands:

- bin/my_app start: Starts the application.
- bin/my_app stop: Stops the application.
- bin/my_app restart: Restarts the application.
- bin/my_app remote: Connects to a running node.

To further automate the deployment process, Continuous Integration/-Continuous Deployment (CI/CD) pipelines can be employed. Services like GitHub Actions, GitLab CI, or Jenkins enable the automation of building, testing, and deploying Elixir applications.

```
name: Elixir CI

on:
  push:
    branches: [ main ]
  pull_request:
    branches: [ main ]

jobs:
  build:
    runs-on: ubuntu-latest

    steps:
      - name: Checkout code
        uses: actions/checkout@v2

      - name: Set up Elixir
        uses: actions/setup-elixir@v1
        with:
          otp-version: 23.0
          elixir-version: 1.11.2
```

```
- name: Install dependencies
  run: mix deps.get

- name: Compile code
  run: mix compile

- name: Run tests
  run: mix test

- name: Build release
  run: mix release

- name: Deploy release
  run: |
    scp _build/prod/rel/my_app/releases/0.1.0/my_app.tar.gz user@server
        :/path/to/deploy
    ssh user@server 'cd /path/to/deploy && tar -xzvf my_app.tar.gz &&
        bin/my_app start'
```

The example workflow illustrates building and deploying an Elixir application through GitHub Actions. It defines steps for checking out the code, setting up Elixir, installing dependencies, running tests, building the release, and deploying it to the server.

Networking and monitoring strategies are also essential for deployed applications. Using tools such as Prometheus and Grafana can help in monitoring the application's health and performance. Configuring alerts ensures that any issues are promptly addressed, improving the application's reliability and availability.

Both security and compliance practices must be integrated into the deployment process. Secure configurations, encrypted communications (e.g., SSL/TLS), and regular security audits are critical in maintaining the integrity and privacy of the application and user data.

A thorough understanding of these deployment techniques ensures that Elixir applications are robust, reliable, and ready for production use. Integrating automation tools and monitoring systems further enhances the deployment process, allowing teams to focus on development and innovation.

Chapter 8

Testing in Elixir

This chapter focuses on testing in Elixir, covering the basics of writing tests with ExUnit and organizing test structures. It includes using assertions and refutations, testing asynchronous code, and leveraging mocking and stubbing with Mox. The chapter also covers property-based testing with StreamData, writing and running doctests, setting up test fixtures, analyzing code coverage, and integrating continuous testing in a development workflow.

8.1 Introduction to Testing in Elixir

Testing is a critical part of modern software development, and Elixir provides robust, expressive tools to support this practice. By introducing testing early in the development cycle, developers ensure that code is reliable, maintainable, and free from defects. Elixir's ExUnit is the built-in testing framework designed to offer a straightforward and powerful means of writing and running tests.

ExUnit tests are organized within modules, where the test cases (individual tests) are defined. Each test case focuses on one specific aspect of the function or module under test. ExUnit integrates seamlessly into Mix, the Elixir build tool, enabling the easy execution and management of tests.

To begin writing tests in Elixir, you must first ensure that ExUnit is started. This can be done by adding a simple line of code in the test helper file (test_helper.exs) located within the test directory of your project.

```
# test/test_helper.exs
ExUnit.start()
```

The test files typically reside in the test directory at the root of the Elixir project. Each test file corresponds to a module's function being tested and should follow a naming convention that reflects this relationship, often by appending _test to the module name.

For example, a module named MyApp.MyModule would have its tests in a file named my_module_test.exs under the test directory.

```
# test/my_module_test.exs
defmodule MyApp.MyModuleTest do
  use ExUnit.Case
  doctest MyApp.MyModule

  test "sample test" do
    assert 1 + 1 == 2
  end
end
```

In the example above, we use the use ExUnit.Case directive to import the ExUnit functionality needed to write tests. The doctest macro is used if you want to include examples from the module's documentation as part of the test suite.

A basic test case is defined using the test macro, which accepts a descriptive string and a block of test code. The assert macro is used to specify expected outcomes.

ExUnit also supports setup callbacks, which are used to prepare the test environment before running each test case. This is particularly useful for initializing shared resources or defining preconditions. Setup callbacks are defined within the setup block.

```
defmodule MyApp.MyModuleTest do
  use ExUnit.Case

  setup do
    {:ok, initial_state: %{}}
  end

  test "sample test", context do
    assert context[:initial_state] == %{}
  end
```

```
end
```

In this setup, the setup block returns a tuple with :ok and a map containing key-value pairs. These pairs are then accessible in the tests through the test context.

Tests may also be organized using descriptive naming to improve readability and maintenance. ExUnit supports grouping related tests using describe blocks:

```
defmodule MyApp.MyModuleTest do
  use ExUnit.Case

  describe "Arithmetic operations" do
    test "addition works as expected" do
      assert 1 + 1 == 2
    end

    test "subtraction works as expected" do
      assert 2 - 1 == 1
    end
  end
end
```

The describe macro helps to encapsulate related tests under a single descriptive heading, making the test output more organized and easier to navigate.

An important aspect of testing in Elixir is the ability to test for failures and exceptions, ensuring robust error handling. This can be done using the assert_raise macro:

```
defmodule MyApp.MyModuleTest do
  use ExUnit.Case

  test "dividing by zero raises an error" do
    assert_raise ArithmeticError, fn ->
      1 / 0
    end
  end
end
```

In this test, assert_raise checks that an ArithmeticError is raised when dividing by zero.

Testing asynchronous code in Elixir is straightforward with ExUnit, thanks to its support for the async: true flag. Adding this flag to a test module allows Elixir to run the tests concurrently, speeding up execution and ensuring that the code handles concurrency issues correctly.

```
defmodule MyApp.AsyncTest do
  use ExUnit.Case, async: true

  test "async test example" do
    spawn(fn -> assert 1 + 1 == 2 end)
  end
end
```

In sum, the ease of setup and the expressive power of ExUnit demonstrate why testing is integral to the Elixir development workflow. The default testing framework supports various testing paradigms, including unit tests, integration tests, and property-based testing, providing a robust foundation for maintaining high-quality Elixir applications.

The next section will delve deeper into writing basic tests with ExUnit, highlighting additional features and best practices for effective test development.

8.2 Writing Basic Tests with ExUnit

Elixir's built-in testing framework, ExUnit, offers an extensive set of tools for writing unit tests and validating your code. This section demonstrates how to write basic tests with ExUnit, focusing on structuring test cases, using assertions, and running tests.

To begin, ensure that ExUnit is started and configured correctly. This is typically done in the test/test_helper.exs file:

```
# test/test_helper.exs
ExUnit.start()
```

The primary building block in ExUnit is the test case, which is defined using the ExUnit.Case module. Let's create a simple example test case in a file named test/example_test.exs:

```
# test/example_test.exs
defmodule ExampleTest do
  use ExUnit.Case

  test "addition works correctly" do
    assert 1 + 1 == 2
  end

  test "string concatenation" do
    assert "Hello, " <> "world!" == "Hello, world!"
  end
```

```
end
```

In the above code, ExampleTest module uses ExUnit.Case to define two basic test functions. Each function is prefixed with the test macro, followed by a description string of the test. Inside each test function, the assert macro verifies that the given expression evaluates to true.

Assertions are a crucial aspect of writing tests. Commonly used assertions include:

- assert expression: Asserts that the expression evaluates to true.
- refute expression: Asserts that the expression evaluates to false.
- assert_in_range value, range: Asserts that the value lies within the specified range.

Consider the following example that demonstrates these assertions:

```
# test/assert_example_test.exs
defmodule AssertExampleTest do
  use ExUnit.Case

  test "assert vs refute" do
    assert 5 > 3
    refute 5 < 3
  end

  test "assert_in_range" do
    assert_in_range 5, 1..10
  end
end
```

Running the tests is straightforward. In the terminal, navigate to the project's root directory and execute the following command:

```
$ mix test
```

This command runs all tests in the test directory and produces a detailed output indicating which tests passed or failed. Here's an example output:

```
..

Finished in 0.02 seconds
2 tests, 0 failures

Randomized with seed 123456
```

The output shows that all tests passed successfully. To execute a specific test file or individual test, use:

```
$ mix test test/example_test.exs
$ mix test test/example_test.exs:4
```

In the first command, all tests in example_test.exs are executed. In the second, only the test located on line 4 is executed.

In addition to basic assertions, ExUnit supports more powerful assertions such as assert_receive and assert_throws for dealing with concurrent and exceptional conditions. For example:

```
# test/advanced_assertions_test.exs
defmodule AdvancedAssertionsTest do
  use ExUnit.Case

  test "assert_receive example" do
    send(self(), :hello)
    assert_receive :hello
  end

  test "assert_throws example" do
    assert_throws :exit, fn -> exit(:timeout) end
  end
end
```

In this example, assert_receive verifies that a specific message is received within the test's process, while assert_throws checks that an exception is thrown within the passed function.

Another aspect of ExUnit is setup and teardown functionality, managed via setup/1 and setup_all/1 callbacks. These functions help prepare the environment before tests run and clean up afterward:

```
# test/setup_example_test.exs
defmodule SetupExampleTest do
  use ExUnit.Case

  setup do
    {:ok, initial_value: 42}
  end

  test "uses setup data", context do
    assert context[:initial_value] == 42
  end

  setup_all do
    IO.puts "Setting up for all tests"
    :ok
  end

  test "another test with setup_all" do
    assert 1 + 1 == 2
  end
```

```
end
```

In this code, setup callback initializes shared data before each test with context passed to the test function. The setup_all runs once before all the tests in the module.

By following the principles and practices discussed here, you can develop a robust suite of tests to ensure that your Elixir code behaves as expected.

8.3 Test Structure and Organization

Test structure and organization are crucial for maintaining comprehensible and maintainable test suites. This section delineates best practices and methodologies for structuring tests in Elixir using the ExUnit framework.

Elixir tests are conventionally organized within the test/ directory of the project. Each module typically corresponds to a test file named with the suffix _test.exs. For instance, tests for a module named MyApp.Calculator would reside in test/my_app/calculator_test.exs. Structuring tests in such a manner promotes easy navigation and clearly delineates the test code base.

Within each test file, the ExUnit.Case module is used to define test cases. The ExUnit.start() function invokes the test process. Here is an example of how one might start a simple test file:

```
defmodule MyApp.CalculatorTest do
  use ExUnit.Case

  test "addition of two numbers" do
    assert MyApp.Calculator.add(1, 2) == 3
  end

  test "subtraction of two numbers" do
    assert MyApp.Calculator.subtract(5, 3) == 2
  end
end
```

Tests are encapsulated within the test macro, followed by a descriptive string and a block of code containing the actual test assertions. Each test macro invocation corresponds to a distinct test.

ExUnit also supports organizing tests into context blocks using the describe macro. Context blocks group related tests, enhancing readability and helping to structure tests logically. Below is an example illustrating context usage:

```
defmodule MyApp.CalculatorTest do
  use ExUnit.Case

  describe "addition operations" do
    test "adding positive numbers" do
      assert MyApp.Calculator.add(1, 2) == 3
    end

    test "adding negative numbers" do
      assert MyApp.Calculator.add(-1, -2) == -3
    end
  end

  describe "subtraction operations" do
    test "subtracting positive numbers" do
      assert MyApp.Calculator.subtract(5, 3) == 2
    end

    test "subtracting with negative result" do
      assert MyApp.Calculator.subtract(3, 5) == -2
    end
  end
end
```

Using the describe macro, tests for addition and subtraction operations are grouped separately, thereby providing organizational clarity.

Test organization also involves incorporating setup and teardown functions which execute setup code before the tests and teardown code after the tests, respectively. ExUnit.Case provides the setup and setup_all callbacks for this purpose. They can be used to prepare any state required by tests.

```
defmodule MyApp.CalculatorTest do
  use ExUnit.Case

  setup do
    {:ok, calculator: %MyApp.Calculator{}}
  end

  test "addition of two numbers", context do
    assert MyApp.Calculator.add(1, 2) == 3
  end
end
```

In the above example, the setup callback initializes a new calculator instance before each test and provides it via the context argument in tests.

For data or state that is used across all tests in the module, setup_all can be employed to execute the setup code only once. Here's a modification showcasing setup_all:

```
defmodule MyApp.CalculatorTest do
  use ExUnit.Case

  setup_all do
    {:ok, calculator: %MyApp.Calculator{}}
  end

  test "addition of two numbers", context do
    assert MyApp.Calculator.add(1, 2) == 3
  end

  test "subtraction of two numbers", context do
    assert MyApp.Calculator.subtract(5, 3) == 2
  end
end
```

In large codebases, managing the configuration of tests becomes essential. One can create a test_helper.exs file in the test/ directory, which is executed before any test files. This file typically includes the initialization of the ExUnit framework, as well as any necessary additional setup.

```
ExUnit.start()
# additional setup
```

Integrating efficient test structure and organization directly contributes to creating a well-managed and predictable testing environment. Incorporating these practices consistently ensures that the test suite remains scalable and easier to understand, thus facilitating greater code correctness and reliability.

8.4 Using Assertions and Refutations

Assertions and refutations are fundamental concepts in Elixir's ExUnit framework, enabling developers to verify the correctness of their code. This section delves into the various assertions and refutations provided by ExUnit, explaining their usage and importance in testing Elixir applications.

Elixir's ExUnit module offers a range of macros to assert that an expression is true and refute that an expression is false. We will explore these macros, focusing on their syntax and practical applications.

The assert macro is used to check if a given expression evaluates to true. Should the expression evaluate to false, the test will fail, and ExUnit will output an error message indicating the failure. The basic syntax for assert is as follows:

```
assert value
```

Here, value is the expression you want to verify as true. For example:

```
assert 1 + 1 == 2
```

If the condition $1 + 1 == 2$ is true, the test passes. However, if evaluating value results in a false value, ExUnit will report an error. Consider the following example:

```
assert 1 + 1 == 3
```

In this case, the assertion fails because $1 + 1$ does not equal 3. ExUnit will output an error similar to:

```
1) test example (ExampleTest)
   test/example_test.exs:5
   Assertion with == failed
   code: 1 + 1 == 3
   left: 2
   right: 3
```

ExUnit also provides the refute macro, which asserts that an expression evaluates to false. If the expression evaluates to true, the test fails. The syntax for refute is similar to that of assert:

```
refute value
```

Here, value represents the expression you want to verify as false. For instance:

```
refute 1 + 1 == 3
```

The test passes because $1 + 1$ does not equal 3, thus meeting the condition for refute. On the other hand, if the expression evaluates to true, the test will fail. Consider:

```
refute 1 + 1 == 2
```

In this scenario, the refutation fails as $1 + 1$ equals 2, resulting in the error:

```
1) test example (ExampleTest)
   test/example_test.exs:5
   Refutation with == failed
   code: 1 + 1 == 2
   left: 2
   right: 2
```

ExUnit provides additional macros to handle more complex assert and refute scenarios. Some of these include assert_raise, assert_receive, refute_receive, and others.

The assert_raise macro is useful for asserting that a specific exception is raised within a block of code. The syntax is as follows:

```
assert_raise expected_exception, message, fn ->
  # code that raises the exception
end
```

For example, to assert that a division by zero raises an ArithmeticError, you can write:

```
assert_raise ArithmeticError, fn ->
  1 / 0
end
```

The test will pass if ArithmeticError is raised; otherwise, it will fail.

assert_receive and refute_receive macros are used in the context of message passing. These macros allow you to assert or refute the receipt of messages within a specified period. The usage for assert_receive is:

```
assert_receive message_pattern, timeout
```

Here, message_pattern is the pattern you expect to receive, and timeout is the duration (in milliseconds) to wait for the message. For example:

```
send self(), :hello
assert_receive :hello, 1000
```

This test passes if the process receives the :hello message within 1000 milliseconds. Conversely, refute_receive can be used as follows:

```
refute_receive :goodbye, 1000
```

In this instance, the test will pass if the process does not receive the :goodbye message within 1000 milliseconds.

Assertions and refutations are instrumental for validating expected conditions and behaviors in Elixir applications. Leveraging these macros ensures robustness in test coverage, fostering reliable and maintainable code. Understanding their intricacies enables developers to write precise and effective tests, ultimately leading to higher software quality.

8.5 Testing Asynchronous Code

Testing asynchronous code in Elixir presents unique challenges due to the concurrent nature of the language. Elixir's powerful concurrency model built on the Erlang VM allows developers to efficiently manage multiple processes. This section will delve into the nuances of testing such code, providing techniques and examples to illustrate effective approaches.

To write effective tests for asynchronous code, it is crucial to understand the underlying principles of Elixir's concurrency model. Asynchronous operations in Elixir typically involve processes, tasks, and messages. The Task module is commonly used to run concurrent operations.

Consider the following example:

```
defmodule AsyncExample do
  def async_add(a, b) do
    Task.async(fn -> a + b end)
  end

  def await_result(task) do
    Task.await(task)
  end
end
```

This module contains an asynchronous addition function that spawns a new task to perform the addition and subsequently waits for the result. Testing such code requires managing the inherent non-determinism of asynchronous operations. ExUnit provides features to handle this effectively.

Using Task

First, we can write a test that verifies the correct functionality of AsyncExample:

```
defmodule AsyncExampleTest do
  use ExUnit.Case
```

```
  test "async_add/2 returns the correct result" do
    task = AsyncExample.async_add(2, 3)
    result = AsyncExample.await_result(task)
    assert result == 5
  end
end
```

This test engages the async_add/2 function and asserts that the result is correct. However, it is often necessary to test more complex asynchronous interactions, particularly those involving multiple processes and messages.

Testing Process Communication

Processes in Elixir communicate via message passing. A typical scenario involves a process sending messages to another process and awaiting responses. We can test such interactions by using the send and receive constructs.

Consider a process that processes tasks asynchronously:

```
defmodule AsyncProcessor do
  def start_link do
    Task.start_link(__MODULE__, :process, [])
  end

  def process do
    receive do
      {:task, sender, a, b} ->
        send(sender, {:result, a + b})
        process()
    end
  end
end
```

A simple test for this process might look like:

```
defmodule AsyncProcessorTest do
  use ExUnit.Case

  test "process sends back the correct result" do
    {:ok, pid} = AsyncProcessor.start_link()
    send(pid, {:task, self(), 1, 2})

    assert_receive {:result, 3}
  end
end
```

Here, we start the process and send it a message with the task details, including the current process as the sender. We then use assert_receive to wait for and assert the correctness of the reply. This approach ensures that the asynchronous nature of the process doesn't result in test failures due to timing issues.

Asynchronous Assertions

ExUnit also provides facilities for making assertions about asynchronous operations without blocking indefinitely. This is particularly useful when waiting for a condition to become true.

```
defmodule AsyncChecker do
  def check_task do
    # Simulate a long-running task
    Process.sleep(100)
    :task_done
  end
end
```

Testing such time-dependent functionality can be achieved using assert_receive:

```
defmodule AsyncCheckerTest do
  use ExUnit.Case

  test "check_task returns :task_done eventually" do
    assert {:ok, :task_done} = Task.async(fn ->
      AsyncChecker.check_task()
    end) |> Task.await()
  end
end
```

Handling Timeouts

When testing asynchronous code, it is critical to handle potential timeouts appropriately. The Task.await/2 function accepts a timeout parameter, providing control over how long a test waits for a result:

```
test "check_task timeouts if it takes too long" do
  task = Task.async(fn -> Process.sleep(5000) end)
  assert_raise Task.TimeoutError, fn ->
    Task.await(task, 100)
  end
end
```

This test demonstrates how to assert that a task times out if it exceeds the specified duration, ensuring that such behaviors are appropriately tested.

Mocking with Mox

Combining asynchronous operations with mocking can be intricate. The Mox library provides capabilities to create mocks for concurrent scenarios. Suppose we have a module that makes an asynchronous call to an external service. We can mock the service call to test how our module handles different scenarios:

```
defmodule ExternalService do
  @callback fetch_data() :: any()
end

defmodule AsyncClient do
  def fetch_from_service do
    Task.async(fn ->
      ExternalService.fetch_data()
    end)
    |> Task.await()
  end
end
```

A corresponding test can be designed to use Mox:

```
defmodule AsyncClientTest do
  use ExUnit.Case
  import Mox

  setup :verify_on_exit!

  defmock(ExternalServiceMock, for: ExternalService)

  test "fetch_from_service returns mocked data" do
    ExternalServiceMock
    |> expect(:fetch_data, fn -> "mocked_data" end)

    assert AsyncClient.fetch_from_service() == "mocked_data"
  end
end
```

Using Mox, we mock the fetch_data/0 function to return predefined data, allowing us to isolate and test AsyncClient.

This section has demonstrated how to test asynchronous code in Elixir using ExUnit effectively. By utilizing tasks, send and receive constructs, timeouts, and mock frameworks like Mox, we can ensure our concurrent systems are reliable and well-tested.

8.6 Mocking and Stubbing with Mox

In Elixir, testing interactions between modules can be complex when code depends on external services or modules that are difficult to control or predict. Mocking and stubbing provide mechanisms to isolate and test specific behaviors without relying on external dependencies. The Mox library is a tool in Elixir that facilitates both mocking and stubbing, allowing developers to define and use mocks explicitly in their tests.

Mox is a library for defining concurrent mocks in Elixir, aiming to strengthen design and segregation of responsibilities by emphasizing modules' defined and expected behaviors or contracts. By using Mox, developers can ensure that their code interacts correctly with external services or modules according to these contracts without executing the actual interactions.

Mox can be installed by adding it to the mix.exs dependencies:

```
def deps do
  [
    {:mox, "~> 1.0", only: :test}
  ]
end
```

Next, ensure that Mox starts along with your application. Modify the test_helper.exs with the following lines to enable Mox globally:

```
ExUnit.start()
Mox.defmock(MyApp.MockModule, for: MyApp.Behaviour)
Application.put_env(:my_app, :module_to_mock, MyApp.MockModule)
```

Defining Behaviors

To use Mox, you need to define a behavior, an Elixir construct that specifies a set of functions that a module should implement. Creating a behavior involves defining a module with callbacks. For instance, consider a behavior defining functions related to a payment system:

```
defmodule MyApp.PaymentBehaviour do
  @callback charge(amount :: float, currency :: String.t()) :: {:ok, map()} | {:error,
        reason :: String.t()}
end
```

Creating Mocks with Mox

Once you have the behavior, you can create a mock for it. A mock should be defined in the application's test_helper.exs file:

```
Mox.defmock(MyApp.PaymentMock, for: MyApp.PaymentBehaviour)
```

This line instructs Mox to create a mock module (MyApp.PaymentMock) that complies with the MyApp.PaymentBehaviour contract.

Using Mocks in Tests

To use the mock in your tests, you must ensure that the application configuration points to the mock module instead of the actual implementation. Typically, this is done in the test setup:

```
setup :set_mox_from_context
setup :verify_on_exit!

@tag :capture_log
test "successful payment" do
  MyApp.PaymentMock
  |> expect(:charge, fn _amount, _currency ->
    {:ok, %{"transaction_id" => "12345"}}
  end)

  assert {:ok, response} = MyApp.PaymentModule.charge(25.0, "USD")
  assert response["transaction_id"] == "12345"
end
```

The snippet above shows how a test can specify an expectation using the expect/3 function. It states that when the charge/2 function is called with any arguments, it should return {:ok, %{"transaction_id" => "12345"}}. This use of Mox ensures controllable and predictable interaction during the test.

Stubbing Functions

Stubbing is another essential feature provided by Mox. It allows setting up default return values for mock functions without specifying strict expectations. Stubbing is useful when you want to provide default behavior for functions while still being able to set specific expectations for particular tests.

The difference between a stub and an expectation is that a stub keeps returning the defined value regardless of how many times it is called, while an expectation must satisfy the number of calls explicitly defined.

For instance:

```
MyApp.PaymentMock
|> stub(:charge, fn _amount, _currency ->
```

```
  {:ok, %{"transaction_id" => "stubbed_id"}}
end)

assert {:ok, response} = MyApp.PaymentModule.charge(25.0, "USD")
assert response["transaction_id"] == "stubbed_id"
```

This test shows stubbing in action where the charge/2 function will always return {:ok, %{"transaction_id" => "stubbed_id"}} regardless of how many times it is invoked during the test.

Verifying Mock Expectations

Mox encourages strict verification of mock expectations. It verifies that the expected calls are made exactly as specified, ensuring accountability in interactions:

```
setup :set_mox_from_context
setup :verify_on_exit!

test "expectation verification" do
  MyApp.PaymentMock
  |> expect(:charge, fn _amount, _currency ->
    {:ok, %{"transaction_id" => "exp_id"}}
  end)

  MyApp.PaymentModule.charge(25.0, "USD")

  # This will fail if charge/2 is not called exactly once
  :ok = verify_on_exit!(context())
end
```

Mox immediately raises errors if the expectations are not met, ensuring immediate feedback during the test execution phase. This approach strengthens the reliability of module interactions in the testing phase, providing a robust framework for developing well-tested Elixir applications.

8.7 Property-Based Testing with StreamData

Property-based testing represents a paradigm shift from example-based testing by focusing on the properties that a system under test should always satisfy. In Elixir, the StreamData library facilitates property-based testing, providing a comprehensive framework to generate input data and ensure that the tested properties universally hold across a vast range of cases. This section delves into fundamental concepts and practical usage of StreamData for efficient property-based testing.

To begin, install the StreamData package by adding it to your mix.exs dependencies:

```
defp deps do
  [
    {:stream_data, "~> 0.5"}
  ]
end
```

Execute mix deps.get to fetch and compile the dependencies.

Unlike traditional tests that focus on specific inputs, property-based tests describe broad properties that should hold for various data sets. The essential elements involve the use of generators to produce test data and assertions to validate properties.

Here is a simple property-based test example using StreamData:

```
defmodule ExamplePropertyTest do
  use ExUnit.Case
  use ExUnitProperties

  property "sum of a list of integers is greater than or equal to any individual
       element" do
    check all list <- list_of(integer()) do
      sum = Enum.sum(list)

      for number <- list do
        assert sum >= number
      end
    end
  end
end
```

In this instance, the check all macro leverages the list_of and integer() generators to produce lists of integers. The property we are verifying asserts that the sum of the list is always greater than or equal to any individual element.

StreamData provides a rich set of generators, such as integer(), float(), binary(), and map_of() among others. Custom generators can also be crafted to suit specific testing needs. For instance:

```
defmodule CustomGeneratorTest do
  use ExUnit.Case
  use ExUnitProperties

  defp even_integer_generator do
    StreamData.filter(StreamData.integer(), &rem(&1, 2) == 0)
```

```
  end

  property "even integers are zero modulo 2" do
    check all even_int <- even_integer_generator() do
      assert rem(even_int, 2) == 0
    end
  end
end
```

Here, an even integer generator is defined, which filters out odd numbers from a stream of integers.

To incorporate more complex validation, we can utilize StreamData with stateful systems, which require managing state and side-effects. The following example shows testing a simple counter module that provides incremental operations:

```
defmodule Counter do
  use Agent

  def start_link(initial_value \\ 0) do
    Agent.start_link(fn -> initial_value end, name: __MODULE__)
  end

  def increment() do
    Agent.update(__MODULE__, &(&1 + 1))
  end

  def get() do
    Agent.get(__MODULE__, & &1)
  end
end

defmodule CounterPropertyTest do
  use ExUnit.Case
  use ExUnitProperties

  setup do
    {:ok, _pid} = Counter.start_link()
    :ok
  end

  property "counter increments correctly" do
    check all steps <- list_of(integer(0..10)) do
      Enum.each(steps, fn _ -> Counter.increment() end)
      assert Counter.get() == Enum.count(steps)
    end
  end
end
```

This test starts an Agent-based counter and verifies that multiple increment operations tally up correctly. The setup block ensures the counter is initialized for each test iteration.

Property-based tests can also address more advanced scenarios through complex data structures. For instance, testing whether a custom data structure maintains invariants throughout various transformations:

```
defmodule Stack do
  defstruct elements: []

  def push(%Stack{elements: elements} = stack, element) do
    %Stack{stack | elements: [element | elements]}
  end

  def pop(%Stack{elements: [top | rest]} = stack) do
    {top, %Stack{stack | elements: rest}}
  end

  def empty(), do: %Stack{elements: []}
end

defmodule StackPropertyTest do
  use ExUnit.Case
  use ExUnitProperties

  property "stack operations maintain LIFO order" do
    check all elements <- list_of(term()) do
      stack = Enum.reduce(elements, Stack.empty(), fn element, acc ->
        Stack.push(acc, element)
      end)

      assert Enum.all?(elements, fn element ->
        {top, stack} = Stack.pop(stack)
        top == element
      end)
    end
  end
end
```

In this example, the Stack module has push and pop operations that need to maintain last-in, first-out (LIFO) order. The property-based test sequences push operations followed by pop, asserting that the elements are returned in reverse order of insertion.

Property-based testing with StreamData enhances test coverage by exploring many edge cases automatically, beyond what a developer may manually consider. These tests are valuable in revealing hidden bugs and ensuring robustness of the code base.

8.8 Writing and Running Doctests

Elixir, being a language designed for productivity and maintainability, provides a built-in feature to allow embedding tests within documentation. These embedded tests are known as doctests. Utilizing doctests can enhance your code documentation by embedding executable examples that demonstrate the intended usage of functions and modules. This section covers the detailed process of writing and running doctests, ensuring that your documentation remains reliable and current.

Doctests are particularly effective for illustrating the expected output of functions. They are automatically verified by the ExUnit framework, which helps maintain consistency between the documentation and the codebase.

Writing Doctests:

To write a doctest, include the doctest attribute within your module. A doctest typically starts with an iex> prompt, followed by the function call and its expected output. The main steps involved in writing a doctest are:

- Identify the function that needs documentation with examples.
- Use the @doc attribute to begin the documentation for the function.
- Within the @doc attribute, start an interactive Elixir shell (IEx) session using iex>.
- Write the function call as you would in an IEx session.
- Provide the expected result of the function call directly below the function call.
- Repeat for other examples if necessary.

Consider the following example function:

```
defmodule Math do
  @moduledoc """
  Provides basic math functions.
  """

  @doc """
  Adds two numbers.
```

```
  ## Examples

      iex> Math.add(2, 3)
      5

      iex> Math.add(-2, 3)
      1

  """
  def add(a, b) do
    a + b
  end
end
```

In this example, the documentation for the add/2 function includes two separate doctests. Each doctest:

- Starts with iex> to denote the prompt.
- Executes Math.add/2 with given arguments.
- Specifies the expected result immediately after the function call.

Running Doctests:

ExUnit, Elixir's built-in test framework, is utilized to run doctests. The steps involved are:

- Ensure ExUnit is configured to run doctests by including doctest calls in your test files.
- Run your tests as you would normally using mix.

Create a test file, normally placed under test/ directory, that includes a call to doctest for your module. For the above Math module, the test file math_test.exs would look like this:

```
defmodule MathTest do
  use ExUnit.Case
  doctest Math
end

ExUnit.start()
```

By including doctest Math, the MathTest module declares that the ExUnit test framework should include and verify the doctests written in the Math module documentation.

To run the tests, execute the following command in your terminal:

```
$ mix test
```

If the output matches the expected results specified in the doctests, the tests will pass. Otherwise, ExUnit will indicate which doctests failed, providing details on the discrepancy between actual and expected outputs.

Doctests are particularly useful when used appropriately. They serve as both documentation and tests, offering the following benefits:

- They ensure that your documentation remains accurate and up-to-date.
- They provide examples of usage that are verified to work correctly.
- They help detect when updates to the code alter intended behavior, as doctests will fail if the actual output does not match the documented expected output.

Incorporating doctests into your Elixir modules ensures that your documentation remains useful, accurate, and current. It bridges the gap between maintaining comprehensive documentation and ensuring code correctness through testing. The practice of writing and running doctests significantly contributes to the robustness and reliability of your codebase.

8.9 Setting Up Test Fixtures

When developing complex applications, it's essential to ensure that the tests are repeatable and consistent. Test fixtures help achieve this by providing a way to set up a known environment before a test is run. In Elixir, setting up these test fixtures is crucial for maintaining a stable and reliable test suite.

To set up test fixtures in Elixir, we utilize the setup and setup_all callbacks provided by the ExUnit test framework. The setup callback is used to run code before each test, while the setup_all callback runs once before all tests in the test case. Using these callbacks effectively can significantly improve the maintainability and reliability of your tests.

```
defmodule MyApp.UserTest do
  use ExUnit.Case
```

```
  alias MyApp.Accounts

  setup do
    # Setup a dummy user before each test
    {:ok, user} = Accounts.create_user(%{name: "Jane Doe", email: "
        jane@example.com"})
    {:ok, user: user}
  end

  test "the user is correctly created", %{user: user} do
    assert user.name == "Jane Doe"
    assert user.email == "jane@example.com"
  end

  test "the user can be fetched by ID", %{user: user} do
    fetched_user = Accounts.get_user!(user.id)
    assert fetched_user.id == user.id
  end
end
```

In the above example, setup/1 is defined to create a user before every test. The setup callback should return a keyword list wrapped in an :ok tuple. Each test can then access this setup data via the test context. Using the test context, you can ensure that each test has the necessary environment and data to run correctly.

If shared setup is required for multiple tests, but does not need to be reset for each one, setup_all/1 can be used. This is particularly useful for expensive operations, such as seeding a database or starting network services.

```
defmodule MyApp.ProjectTest do
  use ExUnit.Case, async: true
  alias MyApp.Projects

  setup_all do
    # Seed the database with initial projects; one-time setup
    {:ok, project} = Projects.create_project(%{name: "Project Alpha"})
    {:ok, project: project}
  end

  test "the project is created correctly", %{project: project} do
    assert project.name == "Project Alpha"
  end

  test "the project can be fetched by ID", %{project: project} do
    fetched_project = Projects.get_project!(project.id)
    assert fetched_project.id == project.id
  end
end
```

In some cases, you may want to run custom cleanup code after each test or once after all tests. ExUnit provides on_exit/2 for this purpose. on_exit/2 can be used to register a function that will run after the test or test case has completed, allowing you to clean up resources.

```
defmodule MyApp.TempFileTest do
  use ExUnit.Case

  setup do
    # Create a temporary file for the test
    {:ok, tmp_file} = File.open("temp_file.txt", [:write])

    # Register a cleanup function to delete the temp file after the test
    on_exit(fn -> File.rm!("temp_file.txt") end)

    {:ok, tmp_file: tmp_file}
  end

  test "write to the temporary file", %{tmp_file: tmp_file} do
    IO.write(tmp_file, "Hello, world!")
    assert File.read!("temp_file.txt") == "Hello, world!"
  end
end
```

By properly managing setup and cleanup tasks, you can ensure that your tests run in isolation without inadvertently affecting one another. This encapsulation of test environments using fixtures helps in maintaining correctness and reliability in ongoing code changes.

Furthermore, for complex setup scenarios, leveraging helper modules can keep your tests uncluttered and focused on their primary verification goals. By extracting repeated setup logic into helper functions, your test cases remain concise.

```
defmodule MyApp.TestHelpers do
  alias MyApp.Accounts

  def create_user(attrs \\ %{}) do
    attrs = Map.merge(%{name: "Default User", email: "user@example.com"},
          attrs)
    Accounts.create_user(attrs)
  end
end

defmodule MyApp.AdvancedUserTest do
  use ExUnit.Case
  import MyApp.TestHelpers

  setup do
    {:ok, user} = create_user(name: "John Smith", email: "john@example.com")
    {:ok, user: user}
```

```
  end

  test "custom user setup works", %{user: user} do
    assert user.name == "John Smith"
    assert user.email == "john@example.com"
  end
end
```

Developing a well-organized test suite in Elixir hinges greatly on effectively using ExUnit's setup capabilities. Through a careful setup of the test environment, proper resource management, and leveraging reusable helpers, developers can uphold rigorous testing standards, fostering confidence and reliability in the codebase.

8.10 Code Coverage Analysis

Code coverage analysis is an essential aspect of testing, providing insights into how thoroughly your codebase is being tested. In Elixir, the primary tool used for code coverage analysis is mix test –cover. This command generates a coverage report that highlights which portions of your code are exercised by your tests, allowing you to identify untested paths, ensuring higher confidence in code correctness, and maintaining code quality over time.

To begin code coverage analysis in Elixir, ensure your project is set up with a minimal test suite. We'll start by creating a basic Elixir project with a simple module and corresponding test cases.

Suppose we have an example Elixir module in lib/math.ex:

```
defmodule Math do
  @moduledoc """
  Provides basic math operations.
  """

  @doc """
  Adds two numbers.
  ## Examples
      iex> Math.add(2, 3)
      5
  """
  def add(a, b), do: a + b

  @doc """
  Subtracts the second number from the first.
  ## Examples
      iex> Math.sub(5, 3)
```

```
    2
  """
  def sub(a, b), do: a - b

  @doc """
  Multiplies two numbers.
  ## Examples
      iex> Math.mul(2, 3)
      6
  """
  def mul(a, b), do: a * b

  @doc """
  Divides the first number by the second.
  Returns `:error` if the divisor is 0.
  ## Examples
      iex> Math.div(6, 3)
      2
      iex> Math.div(6, 0)
      :error
  """
  def div(a, 0), do: :error
  def div(a, b), do: a / b
end
```

Now, let's add some tests in test/math_test.exs:

```
defmodule MathTest do
  use ExUnit.Case
  doctest Math

  test "addition of numbers" do
    assert Math.add(2, 3) == 5
  end

  test "subtraction of numbers" do
    assert Math.sub(5, 3) == 2
  end

  test "multiplication of numbers" do
    assert Math.mul(2, 3) == 6
  end

  test "division of numbers" do
    assert Math.div(6, 3) == 2
  end

  test "division by zero" do
    assert Math.div(6, 0) == :error
  end
end
```

With the test cases prepared, you can generate the code coverage report by running:

```
mix test --cover
```

This command produces an output similar to:

```
Cover compiling modules ...
Generated math app
Consolidated protocols written to _build/test/consolidated
...........

Finished in 0.08 seconds
7 tests, 0 failures

Randomized with seed 123456
Percentage: 100.0%
```

To view detailed coverage information, execute:

```
mix coveralls.html
```

This command generates an HTML report, generally located in the cover directory within your project. Open the index.html file to review visually which lines of your code are covered by tests.

Analyzing the coverage report, pay particular attention to any uncovered lines or functions. Consider the following best practices to improve coverage:

- **Review and Expand Test Cases**: Ensure all branches of logic are tested, including edge cases and error conditions.
- **Refactor Unreachable Code**: Remove or refactor code that is not reachable.
- **Maintain High Coverage**: Aim for consistently high coverage while balancing the time investment required for covering low-risk or trivial code.

Let's address a hypothetical scenario where code coverage might indicate that certain branches of a function are not covered. For example, if tests missed the division by zero case previously, it will be reflected in the coverage report, indicating the necessity to add or expand test cases.

The excoveralls library provides an extended capability for code coverage analysis and integration with CI tools, such as Travis CI or GitHub Actions. To include excoveralls in your project, add it to your mix.exs:

```
defp deps do
  [
    {:excoveralls, "~> 0.10", only: :test}
  ]
end
```

Next, configure excoveralls in your mix.exs to specify how the coverage reports are generated:

```
def project do
  [
    app: :math,
    version: "0.1.0",
    elixir: "~> 1.10",
    start_permanent: Mix.env() == :prod,
    deps: deps(),
    test_coverage: [tool: ExCoveralls],
    preferred_cli_env: [
      "coveralls": :test,
      "coveralls.detail": :test,
      "coveralls.post": :test,
      "coveralls.html": :test
    ]
  ]
end
```

Now, running mix coveralls will produce a coverage report:

```
mix coveralls
```

The excoveralls output includes detailed line-by-line coverage, making it easier to spot gaps in testing. For continuous integration setups, you can add an excoveralls task to your .travis.yml or GitHub Actions workflow to automatically run and verify code coverage as part of your CI pipeline.

The practical application of code coverage analysis in Elixir, combined with the usage of tools like excoveralls, ensures a systematic approach to maintaining high code quality, ultimately leading to robust, reliable Elixir applications

8.11 Continuous Integration and Automated Testing

Continuous Integration (CI) and Automated Testing are pivotal in modern software development practices, ensuring that code changes are continuously tested and integrated into the existing code base with minimal friction. In Elixir, these practices can be smoothly implemented, allowing for robust and reliable software development.

Continuous Integration is a software engineering practice where members of a development team integrate their work frequently, leading to multiple integrations per day. Each integration is verified by an automated build (including test) to detect integration errors as quickly as possible. Employing a CI server is crucial in achieving seamless integration and testing.

Automated Testing involves executing tests automatically every time the code base changes, ensuring that new changes do not break existing functionality. This approach minimizes human error and enhances the reliability of the code.

- CI Services: Common CI services include Travis CI, CircleCI, GitHub Actions, and GitLab CI/CD. These services provide platforms where Elixir projects can be tested automatically.
- Configuration: CI services use configuration files to specify the setup and execution of tests. Typically, for Elixir projects, these configurations involve specifying the version of Elixir, dependencies, and the commands to run tests.

Example: Setting up GitHub Actions for Elixir

Consider setting up a CI workflow for an Elixir project using GitHub Actions. The following is a step-by-step guide:

1. Create a directory for GitHub Actions workflows:

```
mkdir -p .github/workflows
```

2. Create a YAML file for the workflow, e.g., elixir.yml, in the .github/workflows directory. The file should contain the following configuration:

```
name: Elixir CI

on:
```

```
  push:
    branches:
      - main
  pull_request:
    branches:
      - main

jobs:
  build:
    runs-on: ubuntu-latest

    strategy:
      matrix:
        elixir: [1.11.3]
        otp: [23.1]

    steps:
    - uses: actions/checkout@v2
    - name: Set up Elixir
      uses: actions/setup-elixir@v1
      with:
        elixir-version: ${{ matrix.elixir }}
        otp-version: ${{ matrix.otp }}
    - run: mix deps.get
    - run: mix compile --warnings-as-errors
    - run: mix test
```

This YAML file configures GitHub Actions to run specified commands whenever code is pushed to the main branch or a pull request is made to the main branch. The matrix strategy allows testing against different versions of Elixir and Erlang/OTP. The steps section includes checking out the code, setting up Elixir, fetching dependencies, compiling the code, and running tests.

Advanced Configuration

To extend the CI configuration, consider adding additional steps such as code coverage analysis using tools like excoveralls.

1. Add excoveralls to the mix.exs dependencies:

```
defp deps do
  [
    {:excoveralls, "~> 0.14", only: :test},
    # other dependencies
  ]
end
```

2. Configure excoveralls in the test/test_helper.exs:

```
ExUnit.start()
```

```
ExCoveralls.start()
```

3. Add a code coverage step to the GitHub Actions workflow:

```
- run: mix coveralls.github
```

Benefits of CI and Automated Testing

- Early Detection of Issues: CI and automated testing detect issues soon after they are introduced, reducing the time needed to fix bugs.
- High Code Quality: Continuous testing ensures that each integration maintains the integrity of the code base.
- Increased Developer Productivity: Automation reduces the manual effort required for testing, allowing developers to focus on writing code.
- Consistency: Automated tests run the same way every time, eliminating inconsistencies that might occur with manual testing.
- Fast Feedback: Developers receive quick feedback about the status of their code, enabling faster iteration cycles.

Best Practices

- Write comprehensive tests: Ensure that all critical parts of your application are covered by tests.
- Integrate regularly: Merge code changes into the main branch regularly to minimize integration conflicts.
- Automate as much as possible: Take advantage of CI tools to automate testing, linting, and deployment processes.
- Monitor CI builds: Regularly monitor CI build results to promptly address any failures.
- Refactor tests: Keep your tests maintainable and up-to-date with changes in the code base.

Effective CI and automated testing practices lead to a more reliable, maintainable, and scalable code base, aligning with the agile methodologies and rapid development cycles characteristic of modern software engineering.

Chapter 9

Metaprogramming and Macros

This chapter delves into metaprogramming and macros in Elixir. It explains the Elixir Abstract Syntax Tree (AST) and how to write simple macros using quote and unquote. The chapter covers macro hygiene and techniques for debugging macros. It also explores creating domain-specific languages (DSLs), best practices in metaprogramming, case studies, and performance considerations to ensure efficient and maintainable code.

9.1 Introduction to Metaprogramming

Metaprogramming in Elixir refers to the practice of writing code that can produce and manipulate other code during compilation. This capability allows developers to extend the language, create maintainable abstractions, and implement domain-specific languages (DSLs). Understanding metaprogramming is crucial to fully harnessing the power of Elixir.

In Elixir, metaprogramming is primarily achieved via macros, which are special constructs that enable the transformation of the Abstract Syntax Tree (AST) before the code is evaluated and compiled. The AST is a representation of the code as a tree structure, where each node is an operation or value. Metaprogramming operates on this level, enabling the modification of code in a highly flexible and powerful manner.

Macros in Elixir are written using the quote and unquote constructs. The quote construct converts code into its AST representation, while unquote allows for the injection of expressions into an AST. This approach provides the foundation for creating complex and dynamic code transformations.

To begin with, let's examine a simple example of using quote and unquote:

```
iex> quoted = quote do: 1 + 2
{:__block__, [], [1 + 2]}
iex> unquote(quoted)
3
```

In this example, the quote construct takes the expression $1 + 2$ and converts it into its AST representation. When this quoted expression is unquoted, it evaluates back to 3. This basic example illustrates the fundamental process of creating and manipulating code at the AST level in Elixir.

The power of metaprogramming comes from the ability to write macros, which are functions that generate and transform code before it is compiled. Macros in Elixir are defined using the defmacro construct. Here is a simple example of a macro that conditions on a value:

```
defmodule MyMacros do
  defmacro unless(expression, do: block) do
    quote do
      if !unquote(expression), do: unquote(block)
    end
  end
end
```

In the MyMacros module, the unless macro is defined. This macro evaluates the given expression, and if the expression evaluates to false, it executes the block.

To understand its usage, consider the following:

```
iex> require MyMacros
iex> MyMacros.unless 1 == 1 do
...> IO.puts "This will not be printed"
...> end
```

Since $1 == 1$ evaluates to true, the block containing IO.puts is not executed.

While macros provide powerful features, they should be used judiciously. Excessive use of macros can lead to code that is difficult to read, debug, and maintain. Therefore, it is important to follow best practices and ensure that macros are:

- Clear: The intention of the macro should be obvious.
- Isolated: Macros should perform one specific task.
- Documented: Comprehensive documentation is essential.

In addition to these guidelines, macro hygiene is a fundamental concept that must be understood and adhered to. Macro hygiene refers to the practice of ensuring that macros do not unintentionally capture or overwrite variables in the calling context. Proper use of quote and unquote helps maintain this isolation and ensures that the macros do not introduce subtle bugs into the code.

Understanding and implementing metaprogramming and macros requires a solid grasp of the Elixir AST and the mechanisms for code transformation. This chapter aims to provide detailed insights into these concepts, allowing developers to leverage metaprogramming effectively in their projects.

By mastering metaprogramming in Elixir, developers can write more efficient, dynamic, and maintainable code, ultimately enhancing their ability to create robust and innovative applications.

9.2 Understanding the Elixir AST (Abstract Syntax Tree)

The Abstract Syntax Tree (AST) is a crucial concept in metaprogramming within Elixir. It represents the structure of your code in a tree-like format, where each node corresponds to a construct occurring in the source code. Understanding the AST is foundational for writing macros and manipulating code dynamically.

Elixir source code gets compiled into the Abstract Syntax Tree before further transformations and execution. Knowing the structure and components of the AST allows developers to generate and manipulate Elixir code programmatically.

Elixir employs a three-element tuple to represent the majority of its AST nodes. The general form of this tuple is as follows:

$$\{\langle\text{function name}\rangle, \langle\text{metadata}\rangle, \langle\text{arguments}\rangle\}$$

Here, the function name is often an atom, the metadata is a keyword list containing line numbers and other relevant information, and the arguments is a list of sub-expressions.

Basic AST Representation

Let's illustrate with an example. Consider a simple addition operation in Elixir:

```
1 + 2
```

We can view its AST representation using the Macro.to_string/2 function:

```
iex> Macro.to_string(quote do: 1 + 2)
"1 + 2"
```

The quote/2 function converts the expression into its AST representation:

```
iex> quote do: 1 + 2
{:+, [context: Elixir, import: Kernel], [1, 2]}
```

This tuple tells us that the AST for the expression $1 + 2$ consists of the operator :+, some metadata, and two integer arguments 1 and 2.

Quoting and Unquoting

The quote and unquote constructs in Elixir are essential for working with the AST. The quote Macro captures the syntax tree of the provided expression, while unquote allows injection of values or expressions into a quoted structure.

Example of Using Quote and Unquote

Suppose we want to generate a complex expression dynamically. We might do the following:

```
iex> macro = quote do: 3 * (4 + 5)
```

This results in the following AST:

```
iex> Macro.to_string(macro)
"3 * (4 + 5)"
```

```
iex> macro
{
  :*,
  [context: Elixir, import: Kernel],
  [
    3,
    {
      :+,
      [context: Elixir, import: Kernel],
      [4, 5]
    }
  ]
}
```

By observing the nested structure, we see that the tree accurately represents the algebraic hierarchy inherent in the original expression.

AST in Function Definitions

Consider another example where we define a simple function:

```
defmodule Example do
  def add(a, b) do
    a + b
  end
end
```

We can explore the AST using the quote function:

```
iex> quote do
...> defmodule Example do
...> def add(a, b) do
...> a + b
...> end
...> end
```

The corresponding AST is slightly more complex than a simple addition:

```
{
  :defmodule,
  [context: Elixir, import: Kernel],
  [
    {:__aliases__, [alias: false], [:Example]},
    [
      do: {
        :def,
        [context: Elixir, import: Kernel],
        [
          {:add, [context: Elixir], [{:a, [], Elixir}, {:b, [], Elixir}]},
          [
            do: {:+, [context: Elixir, import: Kernel], [{:a, [], Elixir}, {:b, [], Elixir
                }]}
```

```
            ]
          ]
        }
      ]
    ]
}
```

The first element, :defmodule, followed by metadata and the module's content, encapsulates the core elements: the Example module and its add function with parameters and a body constituting the addition operation.

Inspecting AST with Macro

Elixir provides the Macro module to facilitate AST introspection and manipulation. One commonly used function is Macro.expand/2, which recursively expands macros in the given AST node.

Example: Inspecting Macro Expansion

For example, let's inspect the expansion of a pipeline operator (|>):

```
iex> quoted = quote do: "Hello" |> String.upcase
{
  :|,
  [context: Elixir, import: Kernel],
  [
    "Hello",
    {
      :".",
      [line: 1],
      [
        {:__aliases__, [alias: false], [:String]},
        :upcase,
        []
      ]
    }
  ]
}
```

Using AST in Metaprogramming

Grasping the Abstract Syntax Tree allows for precision in metaprogramming tasks. You can define macros that modify or generate code in AST form, ensuring syntactical correctness and facilitating complex code transformations.

Elixir's tooling around AST, such as Code.string_to_quoted/2 and Code.eval_quoted/3, enables further exploration and evaluation of dynamically constructed code.

Analyzing and manipulating the AST forms the foundation of advanced metaprogramming, contributing to powerful and flexible code generation, manipulation, and analysis capabilities. Through this, Elixir ensures robust, maintainable, and extensible systems.

9.3 Writing Simple Macros

In Elixir, macros enable us to perform metaprogramming by allowing us to transform and generate code at compile time. This capability is crucial for creating domain-specific languages (DSLs), simplifying repetitive code patterns, and optimizing performance.

A macro in Elixir is written using the defmacro keyword. To understand how to write simple macros, it is essential to grasp the basic structure and components of a macro definition.

Defining a Basic Macro

A simple example of a macro is one that adds logging functionality to a given piece of code. Let's start by defining a macro that logs the execution time of a function:

```
defmodule LoggerMacro do
  defmacro log_execution_time(do: block) do
    quote do
      start_time = :os.system_time(:millisecond)
      result = unquote(block)
      end_time = :os.system_time(:millisecond)
      elapsed_time = end_time - start_time
      IO.puts("Execution time: #{elapsed_time} ms")
      result
    end
  end
end
```

defmacro defines a macro named log_execution_time. The macro takes a keyword list with a key do and assigns the associated block of code to block. Within the macro body, we use the quote keyword to generate the Abstract Syntax Tree (AST) for the provided block. The unquote keyword interpolates the block into the quoted expression, enabling the execution of the provided code during macro expansion.

Let's break down the macro step by step:

- start_time captures the current system time in milliseconds before executing the block.

- The provided block is executed, and its result is stored in the variable result.
- end_time captures the current system time in milliseconds after the block execution.
- The elapsed time is calculated by subtracting start_time from end_time.
- A message with the execution time is printed using IO.puts.
- Finally, the result of the block execution is returned.

Using the Macro

To use the log_execution_time macro, we need to import it into the desired module and invoke it:

```
defmodule ExampleUsage do
  import LoggerMacro

  def example_function do
    log_execution_time do
      :timer.sleep(1000) # Simulating a time-consuming task
      "Task completed"
    end
  end
end
```

In this example, the example_function calls the log_execution_time macro, passing a block of code that simulates a time-consuming task using :timer.sleep(1000). When example_function is executed, it will log the execution time of the block to the console:

```
Execution time: 1000 ms
```

Macro with Arguments

Macros can also take arguments, allowing you to create more versatile and reusable code structures. Here is an example of defining and using a macro with arguments:

```
defmodule MathMacros do
  defmacro add(a, b) do
    quote do
      unquote(a) + unquote(b)
    end
  end
end
```

```
defmodule ExampleMath do
  import MathMacros

  def perform_addition do
    add(2, 3)
  end
end
```

In this case, add is a macro that takes two arguments, a and b. The quote block generates an AST that represents the addition of the two arguments. When the macro is invoked in perform_addition, it expands to the sum of 2 and 3, producing the result 5.

Macro with Pattern Matching

Elixir macros can leverage pattern matching to handle different input structures effectively. Consider a scenario where we need to define a macro that can work with both single and multiple values:

```
defmodule ConditionalMacros do
  defmacro unless(condition, do: block) do
    quote do
      if !unquote(condition) do
        unquote(block)
      end
    end
  end
end

defmodule ExampleConditional do
  import ConditionalMacros

  def check_value(val) do
    unless val == 0 do
      IO.puts("Value is non-zero")
    end
  end
end
```

The unless macro checks if a condition is false and executes the block if the condition is false. The if construct within the quote block evaluates the negated condition using !unquote(condition). This way, we can introduce conditional logic in a more readable form.

When the check_value function is called with a non-zero value, it will print the message "Value is non-zero" to the console.

ExampleMath.perform_addition() when called, will evaluate to:

5

Using macros effectively can significantly enhance the expressiveness and maintainability of Elixir code. By abstracting repetitive or complex patterns into reusable macros, developers can write more concise and readable code that seamlessly integrates with the language's syntax and semantics. Understanding and mastering simple macro definitions pave the way toward more advanced metaprogramming techniques in Elixir.

9.4 Using Quote and Unquote

In Elixir, the quote and unquote constructs are essential for manipulating and transforming code at the macro level. These constructs allow developers to interact directly with the Elixir Abstract Syntax Tree (AST), enabling dynamic code generation and metaprogramming capabilities.

The quote function takes in code and returns its representation as an abstract syntax tree. This allows developers to see and manipulate the code before it is executed. For instance, quoting a simple expression like $1 + 2$ translates it into its AST form:

```
quoted = quote do
  1 + 2
end
IO.inspect(quoted)
```

The output of the above code is:

```
{:+, [context: Elixir, import: Kernel], [1, 2]}
```

This output shows that the quoted expression is represented as a tuple containing the operator :+, metadata, and the operands 1 and 2. Understanding this structure is critical for creating and manipulating macros.

To alter or inject values into quoted code, the unquote function is used. It allows us to execute and insert code into a quoted expression. For example:

```
x = 2
quoted = quote do
  1 + unquote(x)
end
IO.inspect(quoted)
```

The output will be:

```
{:+, [context: Elixir, import: Kernel], [1, 2]}
```

Here, the variable x is unquoted and its value 2 is inserted into the quoted expression. This dynamic insertion capability is instrumental in writing adaptive and reusable macros.

Another example illustrates how more complex expressions can be built using quote and unquote:

```
defmodule Math do
  defmacro calculate do
    quote do
      x = 5
      y = 10
      result = unquote(x) + unquote(y)
    end
  end
end

require Math
Math.calculate()
```

In this example, the macro calculate defines an expression where x and y are statically assigned within the quoted block. However, it is possible to dynamically inject values into these variables using unquote.

Further enhancing our understanding, consider the case where nested quotes and unquotes are employed:

```
value = 8
quoted = quote do
  a = 1
  b = unquote(quote do value end)
  a + b
end

IO.inspect(quoted)
```

The output will be:

```
{:__block__, [],
 [{:=, [context: Elixir, import: Kernel], [{:a, [], Elixir}, 1]},
  {:=, [context: Elixir, import: Kernel], [{:b, [], Elixir}, {:value, [], Elixir}]},
  {:+, [context: Elixir, import: Kernel], [{:a, [], Elixir}, {:b, [], Elixir}]}]}
```

Here, we can see that the nested quote within the unquote successfully injects the variable value into the outer quote, showcasing how these constructs can be flexibly composed.

Moreover, unquote_splicing is a variant that allows lists to be inserted in place of another list:

```
list = [1, 2, 3]
quoted = quote do
  [unquote_splicing(list), 4, 5]
end

IO.inspect(quoted)
```

This will yield:

```
[1, 2, 3, 4, 5]
```

Through unquote_splicing, the elements of list are directly included in the quoted list, demonstrating another layer of metaprogramming functionality.

Understanding the mechanics of quote, unquote, and unquote_splicing is vital for mastering macros in Elixir. Mastery of these tools facilitates efficient code generation and the construction of more sophisticated metaprogramming constructs whereby code can be dynamically composed, transformed, and compiled. This foundation underpins the construction of domain-specific languages (DSLs) and other advanced metaprogramming techniques explored further in subsequent sections.

9.5 Macro Hygiene

Macro hygiene is an essential concept in metaprogramming that ensures macros do not inadvertently interfere with the surrounding code. Hygienic macros maintain the lexical scope of their variables, preventing unintended variable capture which can lead to subtle bugs that are difficult to trace. Elixir, like many other modern programming languages, provides mechanisms to enforce hygienic macros through the careful handling of variable bindings.

To understand macro hygiene, it is crucial to first comprehend the problem it solves—variable capture. When a macro expands, it generates code that might introduce new variable bindings or reference existing variables. Without proper hygiene, these variable names can clash with those in the calling context, resulting in unpredictable behavior. Consider the following naive macro:

```
defmodule Example do
  defmacro naive_macro do
```

```
    quote do
      x = 1
      IO.puts x
    end
  end
end

defmodule Test do
  require Example

  def test do
    x = 42
    Example.naive_macro()
    IO.puts x
  end
end
```

In this example, x is defined both in the macro and in the test function. When naive_macro is invoked, it sets x to 1, which unintentionally clobbers the x defined in test. This results in the following output:

```
1
1
```

This output is not as expected; the second IO.puts should print 42 but prints 1 instead because the macro has overridden the variable. This demonstrates a lack of macro hygiene.

Elixir addresses this issue using the var! construct and the Macro.unique_var function. The var! construct ensures that a variable refers to the existing binding outside the macro, and Macro.unique_var generates a unique name at compile time to prevent naming collisions. Here's how we can rewrite the above macro more hygienically:

```
defmodule Example do
  defmacro hygienic_macro do
    quote do
      x = 1
      IO.puts x
    end
  end
end

defmodule Test do
  require Example

  def test do
    x = 42
    Example.hygienic_macro()
    IO.puts x
```

```
  end
end
```

While this looks similar, let's dive deeper into a more realistic and complex macro that handles hygiene using Macro.unique_var and var!:

```
defmodule Example do
  defmacro hygienic_assign(var) do
    quote do
      var = Macro.unique_var(:value, __MODULE__)
      unquote(var) = 1
      IO.puts unquote(var)
    end
  end
end

defmodule Test do
  require Example

  def test do
    x = 42
    Example.hygienic_assign(x)
    IO.puts x
  end
end
```

Here, Macro.unique_var(:value, __MODULE__) ensures that var is uniquely named and will not clash with any variable in the scope where the macro is expanded. The generated output will now be:

```
1
42
```

This correctly reflects the intention behind the macro and the local function implementation. Macro development best practices include ensuring that macros are hygienically correct and generate predictable and non-intrusive code.

When designing macros, it's also vital to understand the context in which they will be expanded. Elixir provides tools not only for maintaining macro hygiene but also for inspecting the context—such as the caller environment—using __CALLER__. This can be critical when macros need context-sensitive behavior, such as generating module-specific functions or attributes.

Proper macro hygiene helps developers avoid bugs and improves code readability and maintainability. It is always advisable to test macros in various contexts to ensure they do not inadvertently capture or clobber variables, preserving the intended lexical scoping.

Advancing in macro hygiene practices, one could also leverage tools and utilities provided by the Elixir ecosystem to audit and refactor code involving macros, reinforcing the robustness of macro utilization and guaranteeing the integrity of larger systems composed of numerous macros.

9.6 Debugging Macros

Debugging macros in Elixir can be a challenging task due to the dynamic nature of code generation and manipulation. Macros operate at compile time, transforming abstract syntax trees (ASTs) before the code is executed. To effectively debug macros, it is essential to understand the tools and techniques that can simplify this process.

One of the primary methods for debugging macros is to print the expanded code. Elixir provides a built-in function Macro.to_string/1 that converts an AST back to its string representation. This helps in visualizing the transformed code, giving insights into what the macro has generated. For instance, consider the following simple macro:

```
defmodule DebugExample do
  defmacro debug_macro(expression) do
    IO.puts("Expanding macro with expression: \#{Macro.to_string(expression)}
        ")
    quote do
      IO.inspect(unquote(expression))
    end
  end
end
```

In this example, Macro.to_string/1 is used within the macro to print the expression being passed to it. When debug_macro/1 is invoked, it outputs the expression, enabling the developer to trace the input to the macro.

Another useful tool for debugging macros is the expand/2 function in the Code module. It performs a single expansion of a given macro call, useful for step-by-step inspection of nested macros. The expand_-once/2 function can also be used for partial expansion. This technique aids in isolating problems by narrowing down where an unexpected transformation may be occurring. Here is an example:

```
defmodule StepDebug do
```

```
  defmacro step_macro(expression) do
    expanded = Code.expand(expression, __ENV__)
    IO.puts("Expanded code: \#{Macro.to_string(expanded)}")
    expanded
  end
end
```

In this context, Code.expand/2 expands the expression once and prints the output. This approach is beneficial for debugging complex macros that include other macro calls within them.

Using the IO.inspect/2 function in conjunction with unquote/2 is another practical strategy for examining variables and intermediate results within a macro. By inspecting the values at different stages, developers can understand how each part of the macro is evaluated and transformed. For example:

```
defmodule InspectDebug do
  defmacro inspect_macro(var) do
    quote do
      result = unquote(var)
      IO.inspect(result, label: "Variable inside macro")
      result
    end
  end
end
```

Here, IO.inspect/2 provides a labeled print of the inspected variable, facilitating debugging by revealing the internal state during macro expansion.

In some cases, it may be necessary to invoke the quote and unquote constructs manually to decipher complex expressions and transformations. By breaking down the macro into smaller components and printing their intermediate representations, developers can isolate specific issues. For example:

```
defmodule ManualDebug do
  defmacro manual_debug(var) do
    quoted_var = quote do: unquote(var)
    IO.puts("Quoted variable: \#{Macro.to_string(quoted_var)}")

    transformed_var = quote do
      transformed = unquote(var) * 2
      IO.inspect(transformed, label: "Transformed variable")
    end
    IO.puts("Transformed code: \#{Macro.to_string(transformed_var)}")

    transformed_var
```

```
  end
end
```

In this code snippet, the macro first quotes the variable and prints it. Then it proceeds to transform the variable, printing both the intermediate AST and the final expression.

Developers should also leverage Elixir's compile-time error messages to debug macros. When metaprogramming errors occur, inspecting the stack trace can reveal where the problem originated. Careful attention to error messages helps in pinpointing issues related to incorrect AST manipulation, unquoted variables, or invalid syntax.

For comprehensive debugging, additional tools such as the IEx (Interactive Elixir) shell can be useful. The IEx session allows testing and expansion of macros in real-time, providing immediate feedback and enabling interactive debugging. For instance, using the iex prompt, developers can dynamically expand and inspect macros as follows:

```
iex> require DebugExample
iex> DebugExample.debug_macro(2 + 3)
Expanding macro with expression: 2 + 3
5
```

In the above interaction, the macro's debug print statement is displayed, followed by the execution output, confirming the correct behavior.

By combining these techniques—printing macro expansions, using inspection functions, leveraging error messages, and employing interactive shell sessions—developers can effectively debug and refine their Elixir macros. These strategies help in producing reliable and maintainable metaprogramming constructs, ensuring that generated code performs as expected.

9.7 Creating Domain-Specific Languages (DSLs)

Creating Domain-Specific Languages (DSLs) in Elixir can enhance the expressiveness and maintainability of code in specific problem domains. DSLs allow us to define a specialized syntax tailored to particular tasks, facilitating more intuitive and readable code. Elixir's macro system provides powerful tools to define DSLs by leveraging the Abstract Syntax Tree (AST).

A DSL in Elixir typically involves writing macros to create custom constructs. We achieve this by manipulating the AST directly within our macros. The essential steps to create a DSL in Elixir include defining the macro, using functions quote and unquote, and ensuring macro hygiene. Here, we will explore these concepts in detail by creating a DSL for managing configurations.

First, let's consider a simple macro example that helps set configurations for a hypothetical application.

```
defmodule ConfigDSL do
  defmacro set_config(configs) do
    quote do
      Enum.each(unquote(configs), fn {key, value} ->
        Application.put_env(:my_app, key, value)
      end)
    end
  end
end
```

In this macro, set_config/1 takes a list of key-value tuples and creates an Elixir expression that sets these configurations using the Application.put_env/3 function. The quote block generates the AST, with the unquote function used to inject our runtime values into the quoted expression.

To use our new DSL, we can write:

```
import ConfigDSL

set_config(
  database_url: "ecto://user:pass@localhost/db",
  pool_size: 10,
  request_timeout: 5000
)
```

This will set the provided configurations for our application. When this code is compiled, the macro set_config/1 is expanded into a series of calls to Application.put_env/3 with the provided key-value pairs.

Next, let's consider extending this DSL to support nested configurations. By creating a recursive structure, we can manage more complex settings hierarchies.

```
defmodule NestedConfigDSL do
  defmacro set_config(configs) do
    quote do
      Enum.each(unquote(configs), &NestedConfigDSL.put_config/1)
    end
  end
```

```
  defp put_config({key, value}) when is_list(value) do
    Enum.each(value, fn {subkey, subvalue} ->
      Application.put_env(:my_app, {key, subkey}, subvalue)
    end)
  end

  defp put_config({key, value}) do
    Application.put_env(:my_app, key, value)
  end
end
```

This macro recursively traverses nested lists of configurations, allowing hierarchical settings. For instance, we can now write:

```
import NestedConfigDSL

set_config(
  database: [
    url: "ecto://user:pass@localhost/db",
    pool_size: 10
  ],
  http: [
    timeout: 5000,
    port: 4000
  ]
)
```

Here, nested configurations for database and http are appropriately handled by the DSL.

Understanding macro hygiene is crucial in developing robust DSLs. Macro hygiene ensures that variable names within macros do not conflict with names in the calling code. Elixir uses automatic hygiene to manage this most of the time, but certain cases may require the Var or Macro modules for explicit handling.

Consider a case where a temporary variable is required within a macro. This could lead to clashes if the same name is used in the calling code. By using hygienic naming, we can prevent such conflicts:

```
defmodule HygienicDSL do
  defmacro count_configs(configs) do
    quote do
      count = length(unquote(configs))
      IO.puts "Config count: #{count}"
    end
  end
end
```

In this example, the count variable within the macro might conflict with a variable in the calling context. To avoid this, we can use a generated unique name:

```
defmodule HygienicDSL do
  defmacro count_configs(configs) do
    count_var = Macro.var(:count, __MODULE__)

    quote do
      unquote(count_var) = length(unquote(configs))
      IO.puts "Config count: #{unquote(count_var)}"
    end
  end
end
```

Here, Macro.var/2 generates a unique variable tied to the current module, ensuring no naming conflicts.

By integrating these techniques, we can build sophisticated DSLs that enhance clarity, modularity, and expressiveness in our Elixir applications. This capability is vital for large-scale systems where domain-specificity and maintainability are paramount.

9.8 Metaprogramming Best Practices

Metaprogramming in Elixir allows for powerful code transformations and dynamic behavior, but with great power comes great responsibility. This section outlines the best practices to follow to ensure that macros and other metaprogramming constructs are used judiciously and maintainably.

One must always consider readability and maintainability when implementing metaprogramming solutions. Overusing macros can lead to code that is difficult to understand and debug. Guidelines to achieve best practices are as follows:

1. Limit the Scope of Macros: Macros should be used sparingly and only when necessary. Small, self-contained macros are preferable as they localize complexity and reduce the potential for unexpected side effects. Evaluate whether a function could achieve the same goal before opting for a macro.

2. Maintain Macro Hygiene: Macro hygiene ensures that a macro does not unintentionally interfere with the scope in which it is expanded. Use quote and unquote properly to avoid variable name clashes and other scope-related issues. For instance:

```
defmacro safe_sum(a, b) do
  quote do
    a = unquote(a)
    b = unquote(b)
    a + b
  end
end
```

By unquoting a and b, the macro properly separates the variables in the calling context from those inside the macro itself.

3. Debugging Macros: Thoroughly test macros by ensuring that all edge cases are covered. Utilize the Macro.expand/2 function to see how the macro expands at compile time, which can help in identifying issues early. Consider this diagnostic example:

```
defmacro debug_macro(expr) do
  expanded = Macro.expand(expr, __CALLER__)
  IO.inspect(expanded, label: "Expanded Code:")
  expanded
end
```

```
Expanded Code: {:*, [context: Elixir, imports: []], [1, 2]}
```

4. Documentation and Clarity: Macro behavior should be clearly documented. Provide comprehensive explanations of macro usage, expected arguments, and any side effects. Here is an example:

```
@doc """
Calculates the sum of two numbers.

## Examples
    iex> safe_sum(1, 2)
    3
"""
defmacro safe_sum(a, b) do
  quote do
    a = unquote(a)
    b = unquote(b)
    a + b
  end
end
```

5. Error Handling: Handle errors gracefully within macros. Use appropriate compile-time checks to provide meaningful error messages. For example:

```
defmacro ensure_non_negative(number) do
  if number < 0 do
```

```
    raise ArgumentError, message: "Argument must be non-negative"
  else
    quote do: unquote(number)
  end
end
```

6. Performance Considerations: Metaprogramming can introduce performance overhead. Keep the macro-generated code efficient. Avoid introducing complex transformations that could significantly impact compile-time or runtime performance.

7. Testing: Unit tests for macros ensure they function correctly in a variety of scenarios. Write tests that cover common use cases and edge cases.

```
defmodule MacroTest do
  use ExUnit.Case

  test "safe_sum adds two numbers correctly" do
    assert safe_sum(3, 4) == 7
  end

  test "ensure_non_negative raises on negative input" do
    assert_raise ArgumentError, fn -> ensure_non_negative(-1) end
  end
end
```

8. DRY Principle: Macros should adhere to the DRY (Don't Repeat Yourself) principle. Reuse and refactor common patterns into helper functions or other macros to avoid duplication.

9. Avoiding Overuse: Determine when not to use macros. Evaluate if a task truly necessitates a macro or if a function could suffice. Macros bring additional complexity that sometimes may not be warranted.

Adhering to these best practices will ensure that your use of metaprogramming in Elixir remains clean, maintainable, and efficient.

9.9 Metaprogramming Case Studies

This section explores practical case studies that illustrate the power and flexibility of metaprogramming in Elixir. Each case study demonstrates specific techniques and best practices for crafting efficient and maintainable metaprogramming solutions tailored to real-world scenarios.

Case Study 1: Custom Logger

In many applications, it's crucial to log specific actions or events with detailed context. A customizable logger macro can enhance the clarity and granularity of logging without repetitive boilerplate code.

```
defmodule CustomLogger do
  require Logger

  defmacro log(action, details) do
    quote do
      Logger.info(fn -> "Action: #{unquote(action)}, Details: #{unquote(details)}
          " end)
    end
  end
end
```

Usage within a module:

```
defmodule MyApp do
  require CustomLogger

  def perform_action do
    CustomLogger.log("perform_action", "Starting action execution")
    # Implementation of the action
    CustomLogger.log("perform_action", "Action execution completed")
  end
end
```

The CustomLogger module defines a macro to log actions with specified details, thereby avoiding repetitive code and ensuring standardized log formats.

Case Study 2: Database Query DSL

Creating a domain-specific language (DSL) can streamline database query construction, improving code readability and maintainability. This example demonstrates how to build a simple, expressive DSL for defining SQL queries.

```
defmodule QueryBuilder do
  defmacro select(fields) do
    quote do
      "SELECT #{unquote(fields)}"
    end
  end

  defmacro from(table) do
    quote do
      "FROM #{unquote(table)}"
    end
  end
```

```
  defmacro where(conditions) do
    quote do
      "WHERE #{unquote(conditions)}"
    end
  end
end
```

Usage within a module:

```
defmodule MyApp.Query do
  require QueryBuilder

  def get_users_query do
    QueryBuilder.select("*") <>
    " " <>
    QueryBuilder.from("users") <>
    " " <>
    QueryBuilder.where("active = true")
  end
end
```

The QueryBuilder module provides a simple DSL for constructing SQL queries, allowing for clear and concise query definitions.

Case Study 3: Configuration Validation

Ensuring configurations are valid at compile-time can prevent runtime errors and improve reliability. This case study demonstrates a macro that validates certain configuration parameters.

```
defmodule ConfigValidator do
  defmacro validate_config(params) do
    quote do
      Enum.each(unquote(params), fn {key, value} ->
        case value do
          nil ->
            raise ArgumentError, "Configuration parameter #{key} is missing"
          _ ->
            :ok
        end
      end)
    end
  end
end
```

Usage within a module:

```
defmodule MyApp.Config do
  require ConfigValidator

  @config [db_host: "localhost", db_port: nil]
```

```
  ConfigValidator.validate_config(@config)
end
```

This macro checks for non-nil values in the configuration, raising an error if any required parameter is missing, thus preventing misconfigurations from making it to runtime.

Case Study 4: Automated Function Documentation

Consistency in documentation is critical, especially for publicly available libraries. This case study showcases a macro that automatically generates function documentation.

```
defmodule AutoDoc do
  defmacro doc_function(name, arity, doc) do
    quote do
      @doc """
      #{unquote(doc)}
      """
      def unquote(name)(unquote_splicing(Macro.generate_arguments(arity,
          __MODULE__))) do
        # Function body to be implemented
      end
    end
  end
end
```

Usage within a module:

```
defmodule MyApp.AutoDocumented do
  require AutoDoc

  AutoDoc.doc_function(:sample_function, 2, "This function demonstrates the
      use of automatic documentation for a function with 2 parameters.")
end
```

By leveraging this macro, developers can ensure that all functions are automatically documented, maintaining consistency and reducing the manual effort involved in writing documentation.

Case Study 5: Test Data Generation

Generating consistent and predictable test data is essential for reliable tests. This case study demonstrates a macro to generate test data with predefined structures.

```
defmodule TestDataGenerator do
  defmacro generate_test_data(count) do
    quote do
      for _ <- 1..unquote(count) do
```

```
        %{
          id: Enum.random(1..1000),
          name: "Test Name",
          email: "test@example.com"
        }
      end
    end
  end
end
```

Usage within a module:

```
defmodule MyApp.Testing do
  require TestDataGenerator

  def fetch_test_data do
    TestDataGenerator.generate_test_data(5)
  end
end
```

The macro defined in TestDataGenerator generates a list of test data maps, making it easier to prepare test cases with uniform data.

Additional real-world case studies further illustrate the diverse applications of metaprogramming in various domains, showcasing its potential to solve complex problems succinctly and efficiently.

9.10 Performance Considerations in Metaprogramming

When incorporating metaprogramming in Elixir, assessing the performance implications is essential. Metaprogramming, especially macros, introduces additional compiler complexity, which can affect compilation time and runtime efficiency if not used judiciously. This section discusses critical factors and strategies to ensure that metaprogramming practices maintain optimal code performance.

The time complexity introduced by metaprogramming constructs can be primarily divided into two components: compilation time and runtime. Compilation time concerns arise from the increased processing in the Abstract Syntax Tree (AST) transformations, while runtime concerns typically stem from the generated code's efficiency.

To understand the performance implications, consider the translation process in Elixir using macros. A macro essentially expands the given code context into another form, which the compiler then translates into bytecode.

```
defmodule MyMacro do
  defmacro my_macro(ast) do
    quote do
      IO.puts("Processing AST node...")
      unquote(ast)
    end
  end
end
```

During compilation, the my_macro invocation is replaced by the quoted block. While this pattern is useful for code generation, excessive use of macros can slow down the compilation process due to constant evaluation and transformation of the AST.

```
IO.puts("Applying macro...")
# Output:
# Processing AST node...
```

The first critical consideration is to balance the use of macros and functions. Functions in Elixir are generally less costly to invoke at runtime than macros. Macros should be employed primarily for tasks that genuinely benefit from compile-time code generation, such as creating boilerplate or injecting domain-specific behavior.

Avoiding Macro Overuse

Overuse of macros can lead to code that is difficult to understand and maintain, which in turn can indirectly affect performance due to the additional time required for debugging and optimization. It is advisable to follow these guidelines:

- Use macros for code generation tasks that cannot be handled effectively by functions.
- Ensure that macros produce efficient code that does not introduce unnecessary operations.
- Keep the logic within macros minimal and move complex computations to functions.

Macro Hygiene vs. Performance

Macro hygiene prevents variable name conflicts by isolating the macro's scope from the surrounding code. This is significant for maintaining predictable behavior but can sometimes add overhead.

Using the var!/2 function allows deliberate scope exposure but must be managed meticulously to avoid unexpected conflicts:

```
defmodule SafeMacro do
  defmacro safe_macro(expr) do
    quote do
      var!(result) = unquote(expr)
      IO.puts("Safe Macro invoked")
      var!(result)
    end
  end
end
```

```
result = SafeMacro.safe_macro(1 + 1)
# Output:
# Safe Macro invoked
```

While using this approach can sometimes alleviate performance issues by simplifying scoping rules, it introduces the risk of variable conflicts. Ensure thorough testing when using var!/2 and similar constructs.

Efficient AST Transformations

Leverage Elixir's built-in functions such as Macro.expand/2 to understand how macros transform AST nodes. Efficiently designed macros minimize expansion complexity:

```
defmodule ExpansionMacro do
  defmacro expand_macro(expr) do
    expanded_expr = Macro.expand(expr, __CALLER__)
    IO.inspect(expanded_expr)
    quote do
      unquote(expanded_expr)
    end
  end
end
```

Testing macro expansions ensures their optimized performance, especially for complex transformations. The primary goal is to avoid redundancy and ensure that expanded code retains the efficiency of manually written code.

Benchmarking Macros

Finally, rigorous benchmarking is crucial for performance considerations. Use the Benchee or ExUnit.Benchmark library to measure the performance impact of macros under realistic workloads:

```
defmodule Benchmarks do
  use ExUnit.Case
  import ExUnit.Benchmark
```

```
  test "Performance of my_macro" do
    resulting_time = benchmark(1000, do: MyMacro.my_macro(1 + 1))
    IO.puts("Macro execution time: #{resulting_time} s")
  end
end
```

Benchmark results guide optimization efforts, enabling fine-tuning where macros may introduce latency.

In ensuring that metaprogrammed code is efficient, the key lies in striking a balance — leveraging the power of macros to reduce boilerplate while preventing unnecessary performance hits. Employ macros judiciously, rigorously test their expansions, and prioritize clear, maintainable code to achieve both performance and readability.

Chapter 10

Elixir in Production

This chapter covers deploying and maintaining Elixir applications in production environments. It includes building and releasing applications, managing configuration and secrets, and setting up monitoring and logging. The chapter also addresses error handling, performance tuning, optimization, scaling, and load balancing. Additionally, it explores security best practices, maintenance, upgrades, and presents case studies and real-world examples to illustrate effective production deployment strategies.

10.1 Introduction to Production Environments

A production environment is the setting where software applications are executed and accessed by end-users. It involves the live deployment of the application, ensuring that it serves users effectively with high availability, performance, and robustness. The goal is to provide a stable and responsive user experience and align with business, technical, and operational objectives. Understanding a production environment is critical for the successful deployment and functioning of software applications developed in Elixir.

A production environment typically consists of several components including application servers, databases, load balancers, cache systems, and monitoring tools. Each component plays a crucial role in ensuring the overall system's reliability, scalability, and efficiency.

- **Application Servers:** These are responsible for executing the application code and handling user requests. In an Elixir ecosystem, the application server often involves the BEAM (Bogdan/Björn's Erlang Abstract Machine) virtual machine, which runs Elixir applications.
- **Databases:** They store and manage the application data. The choice of the database (such as PostgreSQL, MySQL, or MongoDB) depends on the specific data requirements and workload characteristics of the application.
- **Load Balancers:** These distribute incoming network traffic across multiple servers to ensure no single server becomes a bottleneck, thereby improving the application's availability and reliability. Common load balancers include HAProxy, NGINX, and AWS Elastic Load Balancing.
- **Cache Systems:** These store frequently accessed data in memory to reduce the time needed to fetch this data from slower storage solutions. Examples include Redis and Memcached.
- **Monitoring Tools:** Monitoring tools track the performance and health of the application and underlying infrastructure. Tools such as Prometheus, Grafana, and New Relic are widely used for this purpose.

Deploying an Elixir application into a production environment involves several steps, each requiring careful planning and execution.

Building and Releasing Elixir Applications: The first step is building the application and preparing it for deployment. This typically involves dependency management, compiling the code, and packaging it into a release. Tools such as Mix and Distillery are instrumental in this process. The following `mix` commands are commonly used in an Elixir application build process:

```
mix deps.get
mix compile
mix release
```

Configuration Management: Managing configuration settings is essential to ensure the application behaves correctly in different environments (development, staging, production). Elixir allows dynamic configuration through environment variables and configuration files. For example, using config.exs to define environment-specific settings:

```
use Mix.Config

config :my_app, :database_url, System.get_env("DATABASE_URL")
config :my_app, :secret_key_base, System.get_env("SECRET_KEY_BASE")
```

Secrets Management: Protecting sensitive information such as database passwords, API keys, and encryption keys is critical. Secret management solutions include environment variables, encrypted configuration files, or dedicated secret management tools like Vault.

Monitoring and Logging: Once the application is deployed, continuously monitoring its performance and health is essential. Aggregating and analyzing logs helps identify issues and debug problems. Elixir integrates with various monitoring and logging tools to collect metrics and provide insights.

Error Handling and Reporting: Effective error handling and reporting mechanisms are essential to minimize downtime and address issues promptly. Libraries such as Sentry or Rollbar help in error tracking and reporting.

Performance Tuning and Optimization: Optimizing application performance involves analyzing bottlenecks, enhancing code efficiency, and scaling the infrastructure as needed. This is an iterative process relying heavily on monitoring and profiling tools.

Deploying Elixir Applications: The deployment process includes transferring the build artifact, configuring the production environment, and starting the application. Automated tools such as Ansible, Chef, and Terraform can aid in deployment automation and configuration management.

Scaling and Load Balancing: Scaling involves adjusting the resources allocated to the application based on current demand. Load balancers ensure that requests are evenly distributed across instances. Elixir's concurrency model and lightweight processes make it well-suited for handling a high volume of concurrent connections.

Security Best Practices: Maintaining application and data security is critical in a production environment. Employing encrypted communication, regular security audits, and adherence to security best practices helps protect against vulnerabilities.

Maintenance and Upgrading: Regular maintenance, including updates and patches, is necessary to keep the production environment secure and efficient. Blue-green deployments and zero-downtime upgrades help in minimizing disruptions.

A thorough understanding of these aspects ensures that the applications are ready for production deployment and capable of handling real-world demands efficiently. This section provides a foundation to build upon in subsequent discussions of specific strategies and tools involved in deploying and maintaining Elixir applications in production environments.

10.2 Building and Releasing Elixir Applications

The process of building and releasing Elixir applications involves multiple stages: dependency management, compilation, packaging, and distribution. Each step is vital for ensuring the application runs efficiently and reliably in a production environment. This section will cover the procedures and tools available in Elixir to facilitate building and releasing applications.

Dependency Management is an essential aspect of building Elixir applications. The mix build tool, integral to Elixir's ecosystem, manages dependencies through the mix.exs file. This file specifies the external packages that an Elixir project requires. Dependencies are declared within the defp deps function. Below is an example of a mix.exs file with external dependencies:

```
defmodule MyApp.MixProject do
  use Mix.Project

  def project do
    [
      app: :my_app,
      version: "0.1.0",
      elixir: "~> 1.12",
      start_permanent: Mix.env() == :prod,
      deps: deps()
    ]
  end

  def application do
    [
      extra_applications: [:logger]
    ]
```

```
  end

  defp deps do
    [
      {:phoenix, "~> 1.5.9"},
      {:ecto_sql, "~> 3.6"},
      {:postgrex, ">= 0.0.0"},
      {:plug_cowboy, "~> 2.0"}
    ]
  end
end
```

Compilation in Elixir is managed by the mix compile command, which compiles source files into bytecode that runs on the BEAM virtual machine. During compilation, mix ensures that all dependencies are fetched and compiled correctly. This command can be run from the root of the Elixir project:

```
$ mix compile
```

Upon successful compilation, the project's _build directory stores the compiled files.

Packaging involves creating a release artifact that can be deployed to production. Elixir provides the mix release command to generate self-contained releases. This command packages the compiled bytecode, the Erlang runtime, and other necessary components. Below is the release configuration in the mix.exs file:

```
defmodule MyApp.MixProject do
  use Mix.Project

  def project do
    [
      app: :my_app,
      version: "0.1.0",
      elixir: "~> 1.12",
      start_permanent: Mix.env() == :prod,
      deps: deps(),
      releases: releases()
    ]
  end

  defp releases do
    [
      my_app: [
        version: "0.1.0",
        applications: [
          my_app: :permanent
        ]
```

```
      ]
    ]
  end
end
```

After configuring releases, generate the release using:

```
$ mix release
```

The resulting release artifact will reside in the _build/prod/rel/my_app directory. This directory contains scripts for starting, stopping, and remote shell interactions with the application.

Distribution of the release artifact is the final step. The packed artifact can be transferred to a production server and executed. Ensure the target server meets system requirements, including having the necessary permissions and correct environment variables. The release can be started with:

```
$ _build/prod/rel/my_app/bin/my_app start
```

Each release contains a bin directory with scripts for start, stop, remote_shell, and other control commands.

Integrating *Continuous Integration/Continuous Deployment (CI/CD)* pipelines can automate this process. Popular CI/CD tools such as Jenkins, CircleCI, and GitHub Actions support Elixir. Below is an example of a GitHub Actions workflow for Elixir:

```
name: Elixir CI

on:
  push:
    branches:
      - main
  pull_request:
    branches:
      - main

jobs:
  build:
    runs-on: ubuntu-latest

    strategy:
      matrix:
        elixir: [1.12.0]
        otp: [24.0]
```

```
steps:
- uses: actions/checkout@v2

- name: Set up Elixir
  uses: actions/setup-elixir@v1
  with:
    otp-version: ${{ matrix.otp }}
    elixir-version: ${{ matrix.elixir }}

- name: Install dependencies
  run: mix deps.get

- name: Compile
  run: mix compile

- name: Run tests
  run: mix test
```

Managing dependencies, compiling source code, creating releases, and distributing them effectively ensures that Elixir applications are production-ready. Automation through CI/CD further improves reliability and consistency.

10.3 Configuration and Secrets Management

Configuration management in Elixir involves determining how your application can dynamically adapt to different environments. This is typically achieved through configuration files that specify various parameters and settings. Properly managing configuration and secrets (like database passwords, API keys, and other sensitive information) is crucial for ensuring your application's security and reliability.

In Elixir, configuration settings are conventionally stored in config/config.exs files. Within these files, application-specific configuration can be set using the config/2 function. Here is a basic example:

```
use Mix.Config

config :my_app,
  repo: MyApp.Repo,
  port: 4000,
  secret_key_base: "some_very_secret_key"
```

This configuration can be accessed in your application code using the

Application.get_env/3 function:

```
port = Application.get_env(:my_app, :port, 4000)
IO.puts("Port: #{port}")
```

For production environments, it is critical to avoid hardcoding sensitive data in your configuration files. Instead, you can use environment variables to keep secrets out of source control. Environment variables can be accessed in Elixir using the System.get_env/1 function:

```
secret_key_base = System.get_env("SECRET_KEY_BASE")
```

To integrate environment variables into your configuration files, you can update your config/config.exs file as follows:

```
use Mix.Config

config :my_app,
  repo: MyApp.Repo,
  port: String.to_integer(System.get_env("PORT") || "4000"),
  secret_key_base: System.get_env("SECRET_KEY_BASE")
```

The in-built Mix.Config module also allows configurations to be segregated based on environments. This approach lets you specify different settings for development, testing, and production. Within the config directory, create dev.exs, test.exs, and prod.exs. These files will override the settings in config.exs when running in the corresponding environment:

config/dev.exs:

```
use Mix.Config

config :my_app,
  repo: MyApp.Repo,
  port: 4001
```

config/prod.exs:

```
use Mix.Config

config :my_app,
  repo: MyApp.Repo,
  port: String.to_integer(System.get_env("PORT") || "4000"),
  secret_key_base: System.get_env("SECRET_KEY_BASE")
```

For secret management, it's vital to minimize the risk of exposing sensitive data. Tools such as dotenv, Kubernetes secrets, or cloud provider secret management services can be used. For instance, the dotenv library for Elixir allows the loading of environment variables from a .env file into the application:

First, add the dependency to your mix.exs:

```
defp deps do
  [
    {:dotenv, "~> 3.0"}
  ]
end
```

Then, create a .env file in the root directory of your project:

```
PORT=4000
SECRET_KEY_BASE=some_very_secret_key
```

Load these variables at the start of your application by adding the following:

```
defmodule MyApp.Application do
  use Application

  def start(_type, _args) do
    Dotenv.load()
    # Start your application logic here
  end
end
```

Kubernetes offers another robust solution for secret management, where secrets can be managed with Kubernetes Secrets and injected into pods as environment variables. Create a secret using kubectl:

```
kubectl create secret generic myapp-secret
--from-literal=SECRET_KEY_BASE=some_very_secret_key
```

Then, reference it in your Kubernetes deployment configuration:

```
env:
- name: SECRET_KEY_BASE
  valueFrom:
    secretKeyRef:
      name: myapp-secret
      key: SECRET_KEY_BASE
```

Finally, leveraging cloud-native solutions like AWS Secrets Manager, GCP Secret Manager, and Azure Key Vault allows seamless integration with Elixir applications while enhancing security. These services provide automated secret rotation, granular access control, and auditing for compliance.

By correctly configuring and managing application settings and secrets, you ensure the security, flexibility, and maintainability of your Elixir applications across different environments.

10.4 Monitoring and Logging

In production environments, monitoring and logging are fundamental practices that ensure the health, performance, and security of Elixir applications. Through diligent monitoring, developers and operations teams can gain insights into system behavior, identify bottlenecks, and preemptively address issues before they escalate. Logging, on the other hand, provides a persistent record of application events, facilitating debugging and forensic analysis.

Telemetry is a key feature intrinsic to the Elixir ecosystem, providing a versatile framework for instrumenting code with minimal overhead. The Telemetry library enables developers to collect and handle metrics, exposing critical performance and operational data. An example of defining and executing telemetry events in an Elixir application is shown below:

```
defmodule MyAppWeb.PageController do
  use MyAppWeb, :controller
  require Logger

  def index(conn, _params) do
    :telemetry.execute([:my_app, :page_load], %{count: 1}, %{})
    Logger.info("Page loaded successfully")
    render(conn, "index.html")
  end
end
```

The execution of telemetry events can be monitored by attaching handlers. Handlers consume telemetry events and perform corresponding actions. Below is an example of attaching a handler to log telemetry metrics:

```
:telemetry.attach(
  "log-page-load",
  [:my_app, :page_load],
  fn _event_name, measurements, _metadata, _config ->
    Logger.info("Page load count: #{measurements.count}")
  end,
```

```
  nil
)
```

To enhance visibility into the system, applications can leverage external monitoring tools such as Prometheus, Grafana, and New Relic. Integration typically involves exporting metrics from the Elixir application in a format that these tools can consume. One popular method is to use the PrometheusEx package to expose metrics endpoints:

```
defmodule MyApp.Metrics do
  use Prometheus.Config

  def setup_metrics do
    :telemetry.attach(
      "prometheus-metrics-handler",
      [:my_app, :page_load],
      &handle_event/4,
      nil
    )
  end

  def handle_event(_event_name, measurements, _metadata, _config) do
    Prometheus.Counter.inc(:page_loads_total, measurements.count)
  end
end
```

For robust logging, the Elixir Logger is a built-in facility that provides extensive capabilities to capture application logs. Developers can configure the Logger to various levels (e.g., :debug, :info, :warn, :error) and direct logs to multiple outputs, including console, files, and remote aggregation services. Configuration in config/config.exs may look like:

```
config :logger, :console,
  format: "$time $metadata[$level] $message\n",
  metadata: [:request_id]

config :logger,
  level: :info,
  backends: [:console, {LoggerFileBackend, :error_log}],
  format: {Logger.Formatter, "$time $metadata[$level] $message\n"}

config :logger, :error_log,
  path: "log/error.log",
  level: :error
```

Additionally, for capturing structured logs that can be queried and analyzed by centralized logging systems (e.g., ElasticSearch, Graylog), libraries such as ElixirJSONLogger and LogstashLogger can be employed to format logs as JSON objects:

```
config :logger, :console,
  format: {ElixirJSONLogger, :format},
  metadata: [:request_id, :user_id]
```

In production, it is critical to ensure that log data is not lost, which can be achieved by utilizing log rotation and aggregation solutions. Systems such as Docker with appropriate logging drivers, or Kubernetes logging mechanisms, can be configured to route logs to centralized storage.

Monitoring and logging are the cornerstones of maintaining a resilient and performant Elixir application in a production environment. Efficient use of these tools and techniques stands as a testament to proficient system administration and robust engineering practices.

10.5 Error Handling and Reporting

Effective error handling and reporting are vital for maintaining robust and reliable Elixir applications in production. Proper error handling ensures that unexpected issues do not crash the application, while thorough error reporting allows developers to promptly address bugs and system failures. This section explores strategies and tools for implementing error handling and reporting in Elixir applications deployed in production environments.

Error handling in Elixir leverages the language's robust process architecture and supervision trees. By encapsulating potentially failing code within isolated processes, Elixir allows the system to fail gracefully and recover effectively. The key to this approach lies in the separation of responsibilities: rather than trying to prevent errors, Elixir programs are designed to detect them early and recover appropriately.

```
defmodule ErrorHandlingExample do
  def safe_divide(a, b) do
    try do
      {:ok, div(a, b)}
    rescue
      ArithmeticError ->
        {:error, "Cannot divide by zero"}
    end
  end
end
```

In this example, try/rescue is used to handle potential ArithmeticErrors when performing a division operation. If an error occurs, the function returns an error tuple instead of crashing. This pattern is beneficial for handling specific errors while allowing the program to continue executing.

However, idiomatic Elixir often employs the :ok/:error tuple pattern without using try/rescue, particularly in scenarios where errors are expected outcomes rather than true exceptions. Pattern matching on these tuples helps in making error handling explicit and more readable.

```
defmodule SafeFileReader do
  def read_file(path) do
    case File.read(path) do
      {:ok, content} -> {:ok, content}
      {:error, reason} -> {:error, reason}
    end
  end
end
```

In this example, the function read_file/1 returns an :ok tuple upon successful file reading, and an :error tuple indicating the reason for failure if it cannot read the file.

When designing supervision trees, each process should have a clear and specific role, often encapsulated within a module. Processes that might fail should be supervised by more resilient processes. Supervisors can restart failed processes, ensuring that failure does not propagate unchecked throughout the application.

```
defmodule MyApp.Worker do
  use GenServer

  # Client API
  def start_link(arg) do
    GenServer.start_link(__MODULE__, arg, name: __MODULE__)
  end

  # Server Callbacks
  def init(arg) do
    {:ok, arg}
  end

  def handle_call(:crash, _from, state) do
    {:stop, :normal, :crash, state}
  end
end

defmodule MyApp.Supervisor do
  use Supervisor

  def start_link(arg) do
```

```
    Supervisor.start_link(__MODULE__, arg, name: __MODULE__)
  end

  def init(_arg) do
    children = [
      {MyApp.Worker, [:some_initial_arg]}
    ]

    Supervisor.init(children, strategy: :one_for_one)
  end
end
```

In this example, MyApp.Worker is a GenServer process that can be started and supervised by MyApp.Supervisor. The supervisor's one_for_one strategy configuration ensures that if the worker process crashes, it will be restarted without affecting other supervised processes.

Reporting errors in production is crucial for debugging and maintaining the system. A common practice is to use logging and error tracking tools. Elixir provides efficient logging capabilities via the Logger module. By carefully configuring the Logger, you can capture detailed information about your application's runtime behavior.

```
defmodule MyApp.Handler do
  require Logger

  def process_request(request) do
    case process(request) do
      {:ok, result} ->
        {:ok, result}
      {:error, reason} ->
        Logger.error("Failed to process request: #{inspect(reason)}")
        {:error, reason}
    end
  end

  defp process(request) do
    # Logic to process the request
  end
end
```

In this logging example, when the process/1 function returns an error, the error is logged using Logger.error/1. This log entry can help developers track down the nature and circumstances of errors.

For more sophisticated error tracking, Elixir applications can integrate with external error monitoring services such as Sentry or AppSignal. These tools provide real-time alerts and detailed reports on errors, allowing developers to react swiftly to new issues.

```
defmodule MyApp.SentryHandler do
  require Logger

  def handle_error(error) do
    Sentry.capture_exception(error)
    Logger.error("Captured error: #{inspect(error)}")
  end
end
```

In this example, when an error needs to be handled, the handle_error/1 function logs the error and sends it to Sentry for tracking and reporting.

Leveraging Elixir's robust error handling mechanisms through supervision trees, try/rescue clauses, and process-isolated error management, combined with diligent logging and external error tracking integrations, ensures that applications not only recover from failures gracefully but also provide actionable insights for developers to improve system reliability continuously.

10.6 Performance Tuning and Optimization

Performance tuning and optimization in Elixir applications are crucial for ensuring efficiency, scalability, and responsiveness under various loads. This section delves into multiple strategies and methods to enhance the performance of Elixir applications, focusing on implementing best practices, profiling tools, and optimizing code.

To begin with, it is important to identify performance bottlenecks in the application. Profiling tools such as exprof, eprof, and fprof can be utilized to obtain detailed insights into the execution time of functions and processes. Consider the following example using exprof:

```
defmodule MyApp.Performance do
  use ExProf.Macro

  @profiled true
  def example_function(arg1, arg2) do
    Enum.map(1..1000, fn x -> x * x end)
  end
end

# Profiling the function
ExProf.Macro.__using__(MyApp.Performance)
MyApp.Performance.example_function(1, 2)
ExProf.Macro.profile()
```

The above code demonstrates how to profile a function to identify parts of the code that consume the most resources. Profiling outputs are displayed in a verbose format:

```
Profile results:
#CALLS    TOTAL ( s)  In mSec    BYTES BEAM Unit          FUNCTION
------  ------------  -------   ----- --------------- -------------
   100      10000.0     10.00  32768 range:foreach/3
   100      5000.0       5.00  4096  lists:foreach/2
   100      2500.0       2.50   512  timer:tc/3
```

After identifying bottlenecks, optimization can target specific areas:

- **Concurrency Optimization:** Elixir's concurrency model leverages lightweight processes to handle tasks. Optimize by ensuring that processes are not overloaded and leverage Task.async/await for parallel execution:

```
tasks = Enum.map(1..10, fn i ->
  Task.async(fn -> perform_heavy_computation(i) end)
end)

results = Enum.map(tasks, &Task.await/1)
```

- **I/O Bound Operations:** Implement asynchronous I/O operations in scenarios involving external systems, like databases or APIs, to prevent bottlenecking on I/O waits. Use GenStage for back pressure-aware I/O operations.

- **Data Structures:** Choose appropriate data structures. For instance, prefer Map over Keyword for frequent access operations due to differences in time complexity.

- **Memory Management:** Use the :erlang.term_to_binary and :erlang.binary_to_term functions for efficient memory representation and reduce memory footprint where applicable. Here's an example of using these functions:

```
data = %{foo: "bar", numbers: [1, 2, 3]}
binary = :erlang.term_to_binary(data)

restored_data = :erlang.binary_to_term(binary)
```

- **Garbage Collection:** Monitor and adjust the garbage collection (GC) process by checking the frequency and duration of GC pauses using tools such as :recon.

- **Code Efficiency:** Optimize algorithms and function efficiency by avoiding unnecessary computations and utilizing built-in functions for common tasks. Avoid N+1 queries in ecto, batch database interactions wherever possible.

```
from(u in User, preload: [:posts])
|> Repo.all
```

To measure the impact of optimizations, we run benchmarks using the benchee library. Here is an example to benchmark two sorting algorithms:

```
defmodule MyApp.Benchmarks do
  use Benchee

  @data Enum.to_list(1..1000) |> Enum.shuffle()

  def sort_slow() do
    Enum.sort(@data)
  end

  def sort_fast() do
    :lists.sort(@data)
  end

  Benchee.run(
    %{
      "Enum.sort" => fn -> sort_slow() end,
      ":lists.sort" => fn -> sort_fast() end
    }
  )
end
```

The benchmark results provide quantitative data to aid in decision-making:

```
Benchmarking Enum.sort...
Benchmarking :lists.sort...

Name          ips      average  deviation     median
Enum.sort     500.00    2.00ms   ±2.00%        2.00ms
:lists.sort   700.15   1.43ms   ±1.50%       1.45ms
```

These results indicate that :lists.sort is more efficient than Enum.sort for the given dataset. By applying such detailed profiling and targeted optimizations, Elixir applications can achieve heightened performance and robustness suitable for production environments.

10.7 Deploying Elixir Applications

Deploying Elixir applications involves a series of steps that ensure your application runs smoothly and reliably in a production environment. This section encompasses preparing the deployment environment, creating deployment artifacts, and automating the deployment process.

The initial stage involves setting up the production environment. This may include provisioning servers or utilizing cloud services such as AWS, GCP, or Azure. It is essential to ensure that the infrastructure matches the requirements outlined during the development phase.

Preparing the Deployment Environment

- Elixir and Erlang installation: Ensure the production environment has the correct versions of Elixir and Erlang installed. Consistency across development, staging, and production environments is critical for avoiding unexpected behavior.

- Database setup: The database must be configured and accessible from the application servers. Ensure necessary migrations have been applied.

- Dependencies installation: Non-Elixir dependencies, such as system libraries or third-party services, need to be suitably configured and running.

Creating Deployment Artifacts

The next step is building the application into a deployable format. The most common approach involves creating a release using the mix release command. A release bundles the application, including the Erlang runtime, and produces a set of files that can be deployed to the production server.

```
$ MIX_ENV=prod mix release
```

The output of this command is a self-contained directory including the compiled application, its dependencies, and startup scripts. This directory can be transferred to the production servers for deployment.

Automating Deployment

To ensure consistent and reproducible deployments, automate the process using Continuous Integration (CI) and Continuous Deployment (CD) tools such as GitHub Actions, GitLab CI, Jenkins, or CircleCI.

```
name: Elixir CI

on:
  push:
    branches:
      - main
  pull_request:
    branches:
      - main

jobs:
  build:
    runs-on: ubuntu-latest
    steps:
      - uses: actions/checkout@v2
      - name: Set up Elixir
        uses: actions/setup-elixir@v1
        with:
          elixir-version: '1.11'
          otp-version: '23'
      - name: Install dependencies
        run: mix deps.get
      - name: Run tests
        run: mix test
      - name: Build Release
        run: MIX_ENV=prod mix release
      - name: Deploy to Production
        run: |
          scp -r _build/prod/rel/my_app user@production:/path/to/deploy
          ssh user@production '/path/to/deploy/bin/my_app start'
```

Configuration Management

Configuration files, secrets, and environment-specific settings should be managed carefully. One approach is to use environment variables for sensitive data such as database credentials or API keys. Tools like Docker or Kubernetes provide mechanisms for handling secrets and configurations securely.

Runtime Considerations

Ensure the application can handle the production workload, which may require fine-tuning the runtime settings. The vm.args and sys.config files generated in the release can be adjusted to optimize performance. For example, you might increase the number of schedulers based on the number of available CPU cores:

```
-sname my_app
-setcookie my_secret_cookie
+S 8 % Number of Erlang schedulers
+P 134217727 % Max number of processes
+-kernel inet_dist_listen_min 9100
+-kernel inet_dist_listen_max 9105
```

Final Steps

Before switching the application live, perform thorough testing in a staging environment that mirrors production as closely as possible. This minimizes the risk of deployment-related issues. Once confirmed, the production deployment can proceed.

Transition monitoring to observe the application's performance, leveraging logs and metrics to catch and address issues promptly. Regularly update dependencies and apply patches to mitigate security risks. Adopting best practices ensures optimal performance and reliability for the users.

10.8 Scaling and Load Balancing

Scaling Elixir applications and implementing load balancing mechanisms are crucial for ensuring resilience and performance in production environments. In this section, we will delve into the methodologies and tools available for scaling Elixir-based systems and applying effective load balancing strategies.

When discussing scaling, we consider two primary forms: vertical scaling and horizontal scaling. Vertical scaling enhances the capabilities of a single node by adding more resources, such as CPU, memory, or storage. Horizontal scaling, in contrast, involves adding more nodes to the system to distribute the workload.

Vertical Scaling

In the context of Elixir applications, vertical scaling often involves optimizing the performance of the Erlang VM. Key parameters such as process count, garbage collection tuning, and memory allocation strategies can be fine-tuned.

The +P flag in the Erlang VM can be used to increase the number of concurrent processes that can be run. For example:

```
$ iex --erl "+P 134217727"
```

This command increases the process limit to the maximum allowed value. It is essential when applications have a high concurrency requirement.

Horizontal Scaling

Horizontal scaling can be achieved by running multiple instances of the Elixir application and distributing the incoming requests among these instances. To facilitate this, we typically use an orchestration tool like Kubernetes along with containerization technologies such as Docker.

Here is an example Dockerfile for building an Elixir application:

```
# Use the official Elixir image
FROM elixir:latest

# Install Hex package manager
RUN mix local.hex --force
RUN mix local.rebar --force

# Set the working directory
WORKDIR /app

# Copy the Elixir project files
COPY . .

# Install dependencies
RUN mix deps.get

# Compile the project
RUN mix compile

# Run the Elixir application
CMD ["mix", "phx.server"]
```

To run multiple instances, we could use Kubernetes deployment configurations. Here's a sample Kubernetes deployment YAML configuration:

```
apiVersion: apps/v1
kind: Deployment
metadata:
  name: elixir-app
  labels:
    app: elixir-app
spec:
  replicas: 3
  selector:
    matchLabels:
      app: elixir-app
```

```
  template:
    metadata:
      labels:
        app: elixir-app
    spec:
      containers:
      - name: elixir-app
        image: elixir:latest
        ports:
        - containerPort: 4000
```

This configuration will create three replicas of the Elixir application, enabling horizontal scaling.

Load Balancing

Load balancing is the next step after horizontally scaling the application. A load balancer distributes incoming network traffic across multiple servers, ensuring no single server becomes a bottleneck.

Nginx is a popular choice for HTTP load balancing in Elixir applications. Below is an example of an Nginx configuration file for load balancing:

```
http {
    upstream elixir_app {
        server 192.168.1.1:4000;
        server 192.168.1.2:4000;
        server 192.168.1.3:4000;
    }

    server {
        listen 80;
        location / {
            proxy_pass http://elixir_app;
            proxy_set_header Host $host;
            proxy_set_header X-Real-IP $remote_addr;
            proxy_set_header X-Forwarded-For $proxy_add_x_forwarded_for;
            proxy_set_header X-Forwarded-Proto $scheme;
        }
    }
}
```

In this configuration, Nginx forwards incoming requests to one of the servers in the elixir_app upstream group, ensuring balanced load across all instances.

To further improve the resilience and effectiveness of load balancing, one can employ health checks and circuit breakers. Kubernetes facilitates this via its readinessProbe and livenessProbe features:

```
apiVersion: apps/v1
```

```
kind: Deployment
metadata:
  name: elixir-app
spec:
  replicas: 3
  template:
    metadata:
      labels:
        app: elixir-app
    spec:
      containers:
      - name: elixir-app
        image: elixir:latest
        ports:
        - containerPort: 4000
        livenessProbe:
          httpGet:
            path: /health
            port: 4000
          initialDelaySeconds: 3
          periodSeconds: 3
```

Here, the livenessProbe ensures that Kubernetes checks the health status of the application by hitting the /health endpoint at regular intervals. If an instance fails the health check, Kubernetes will restart it.

Combining horizontal scaling with effective load balancing mechanisms, particularly within a robust container orchestration framework like Kubernetes, provides a scalable and resilient architecture for Elixir applications. By leveraging these approaches, you ensure that your Elixir applications can handle increasing load while maintaining high availability and performance.

10.9 Security Best Practices

In the production deployment of Elixir applications, incorporating robust security measures is imperative to protect sensitive data and maintain system integrity. This section provides a comprehensive overview of security best practices tailored for Elixir applications, focusing on secure coding practices, dependency management, authentication, authorization, encryption, and network security.

Secure Coding Practices

Secure coding begins with adopting defensive programming techniques to prevent vulnerabilities at the code level. Ensure that all user inputs are validated and sanitized before processing. Avoid using hard-coded secrets in your codebase, and utilize environment variables or dedicated secret management tools for storing sensitive information.

For example, instead of hardcoding a database password, use the System.get_env/1 function to retrieve it from an environment variable:

```
db_password = System.get_env("DB_PASSWORD")
```

Use pattern matching carefully to avoid exposing sensitive data or creating unintentional vulnerabilities. For instance, ensure that functions handle unexpected patterns gracefully and do not expose sensitive information in error messages.

Dependency Management

Regularly audit your project's dependencies to ensure they are up to date and free from known vulnerabilities. Use tools such as mix_audit to automatically check for security advisories affecting your dependencies. To install mix_audit, add it to your mix.exs file:

```
defp deps do
  [
    {:mix_audit, "~> 0.1.0", only: [:dev, :test], runtime: false}
  ]
end
```

Then, run the audit:

```
mix deps.get
mix deps.audit
```

This sequence will check for any vulnerabilities and guide you in updating the affected libraries.

Authentication and Authorization

Implement robust authentication and authorization mechanisms to protect your application endpoints. Use the Comeonin and Guardian libraries to manage authentication processes securely. For instance, to use Guardian, add it to your deps:

```
defp deps do
  [
    {:guardian, "~> 2.0"}
  ]
end
```

Configure Guardian to work with your user authentication system:

```
config :my_app, MyApp.Guardian,
  issuer: "my_app",
  secret_key: System.get_env("GUARDIAN_SECRET_KEY")
```

Remember to generate and safely store GUARDIAN_SECRET_KEY using an environment variable.

For authorization, use libraries like Bodyguard to define access control policies. For instance, define a policy module:

```
defmodule MyApp.Policy do
  use Bodyguard.Policy

  def authorize(:admin_action, user, _params) do
    cond do
      user.role == "admin" -> :ok
      true -> :error
    end
  end
end
```

Invoke the policy in your controller or context:

```
case Bodyguard.permit(MyApp.Policy, :admin_action, current_user, params) do
  :ok -> # proceed with action
  :error -> # deny access
end
```

Encryption

Use encryption to protect sensitive data both in transit and at rest. Leverage Elixir's Comeonin and Argon2 libraries for secure password hashing:

```
{:ok, hashed_password} = Argon2.hash_pwd_salt("password")
```

For data encryption, use libraries such as jose for JSON Web Encryption (JWE) and JSON Web Tokens (JWT). Encrypt data before storing it in a database:

```
plaintext = "sensitive data"
{:ok, jwk} = JOSE.JWK.from_pem_file("path/to/private.pem")
jwe = JOSE.JWE.block_encrypt(jwk, plaintext, %{"alg" => "RSA-OAEP", "enc
      " => "A128GCM"})
```

Network Security

Ensure your application is accessible only over secure channels. Use HTTPS by configuring Phoenix to support SSL connections. Update the endpoint configuration in config/prod.exs:

```
config :my_app, MyAppWeb.Endpoint,
  https: [
    port: 443,
    cipher_suite: :strong,
    keyfile: System.get_env("SSL_KEY_PATH"),
    certfile: System.get_env("SSL_CERT_PATH")
  ],
  force_ssl: [hsts: true]
```

force_ssl ensures that all requests are redirected to HTTPS, enforcing strict security measures.

Consider employing Web Application Firewalls (WAF) and Intrusion Detection Systems (IDS) to prevent and monitor potential security threats. These tools provide an additional layer of security by inspecting incoming traffic for malicious activity.

Incorporate regular security audits and penetration testing into your deployment pipeline to identify and address potential vulnerabilities proactively.

10.10 Maintenance and Upgrading

To ensure the ongoing reliability and efficiency of Elixir applications, regular maintenance and upgrades are essential. Proper maintenance practices prevent unexpected downtime and security vulnerabilities, while timely upgrades can leverage improvements in the Elixir ecosystem.

Maintenance of Elixir Applications

Routine maintenance tasks can be categorized into several key areas:

- **Monitoring System Health**: Continuous monitoring of system metrics is crucial. Tools such as Prometheus, combined with Grafana for visualization, allow for real-time oversight of application health.
- **Log Management**: Implement comprehensive logging strategies using tools like the Logger module in Elixir, ELK (Elasticsearch, Logstash, Kibana) stack, or even cloud services such as Loggly. Proper log rotation policies must be determined to ensure logs do not consume excessive storage.

- **Database Maintenance**: Regularly perform backups, index maintenance, and cleanup of obsolete or unnecessary data to ensure database performance and data integrity.
- **Security Checks**: Conduct periodic security assessments and apply patches to handle newly discovered vulnerabilities. Utilize libraries like sobelow to scan for common security issues in Phoenix applications.

Upgrading Elixir Applications

The upgrading process typically involves version changes of Elixir, Erlang/OTP, and dependent libraries. This process can be broken down into several steps to minimize risks:

1. **Review Release Notes**: Start by carefully reviewing the release notes for the new versions to understand the changes, deprecations, and potential impacts on your application. Elixir and Erlang often release detailed notes on their respective changes.
2. **Update Dependencies**: Use the mix deps.update command to update your dependencies. It is crucial to resolve any dependency conflicts that might arise:

   ```
   mix deps.update --all
   ```

   Once updated, make sure to review any changelogs or documentation for the updated dependencies.
3. **Run Tests**: Execute the test suite to detect any issues introduced by the upgrades. If possible, enhance the test coverage to include areas of the application that might be affected by the upgrades:

   ```
   mix test
   ```

   Evaluate test results meticulously and fix any breaking changes discovered.
4. **Refactor Deprecated Code**: Address deprecations by refactoring the codebase to comply with the new standards introduced by the upgraded versions. Look for warnings during compilation and execution for guidance on necessary changes.
5. **Perform Staged Rollouts**: Use strategies such as blue-green deployments or canary releases to deploy the upgraded application. This minimizes the risk by first deploying the upgrade to a

subset of users or environments, thus validating stability before a full rollout.

6. **Monitor and Validate**: After deployment, monitor the application closely for any abnormal behaviors or performance regressions. Tools such as New Relic or AppSignal can be highly effective for real-time monitoring.

Version Management Best Practices

Best practices in version management ensure smooth upgrade processes and maintain stability:

Semantic Versioning (SemVer) is a widely adopted versioning scheme that helps manage software versions through easy-to-understand conventions:

- **MAJOR version**: Incremented for incompatible API changes.
- **MINOR version**: Incremented for backward-compatible functionality.
- **PATCH version**: Incremented for backward-compatible bug fixes.

Adhering to SemVer principles makes dependency management more predictable and reduces the risk of integration issues.

Automated Testing and Continuous Integration

Integrating automated testing and continuous integration (CI) processes is indispensable for efficient maintenance and upgrades:

- Utilize CI tools such as Jenkins, CircleCI, or GitHub Actions to run tests automatically on each change.
- Implement a variety of tests, including unit tests, integration tests, and end-to-end tests, to thoroughly validate the application.
- Automate deployment processes using CI/CD pipelines to ensure consistency and reliability.

Documentation and Code Comments

Clear and comprehensive documentation is vital for maintaining and upgrading applications. This includes:

- Maintaining README files and in-code comments to explain functionality and upgrade procedures.
- Keeping the documentation up to date with changes, particularly with each new release or version update.

Together, effective maintenance and upgrading practices ensure Elixir applications remain robust, performant, and secure in dynamic production environments.

10.11 Case Studies and Real-World Examples

This section delves into real-world scenarios where Elixir applications have been successfully deployed in production environments. These case studies will help solidify the theoretical concepts covered throughout the chapter by showcasing their practical implementation.

Case Study 1: Real-Time Communication Platform

Company: ChatNow

Problem: ChatNow aimed to create a real-time messaging platform capable of handling millions of concurrent connections. The platform needed to provide low latency and high availability with real-time updates.

Solution: ChatNow chose Elixir and its robust, scalable concurrency model powered by the Erlang VM. The primary architecture of the application employed lightweight processes to handle individual user connections, capitalizing on the Erlang VM's ability to efficiently manage thousands of processes.

The implementation involved key components as follows:

- *WebSocket Connections:* Each user connection was managed via WebSockets, allowing real-time, bidirectional communication.
- *Presence Tracking:* The presence of users (i.e., online status) was managed using Elixir's Phoenix.Presence, providing immediate updates to user statuses.
- *Message Routing:* Messages were efficiently routed to recipient users using Phoenix.PubSub for fast message delivery.

- *Fault Tolerance:* Supervision trees were extensively used to ensure fault tolerance, automatically restarting failed processes without affecting the overall system.

Here is a simplified snippet of the WebSocket handler:

```
defmodule ChatNowWeb.UserSocket do
  use Phoenix.Socket

  ## Channels
  channel "room:*", ChatNowWeb.RoomChannel

  ## Transports
  transport :websocket, Phoenix.Transports.WebSocket

  def connect(_params, socket, _connect_info) do
    {:ok, socket}
  end

  def id(_socket), do: nil
end
```

Outcome: ChatNow successfully launched its platform, supporting over a million concurrent users with negligible latency. The use of Elixir's fault-tolerance and scalability features ensured high availability and performance.

Case Study 2: E-Commerce Platform

Company: ShopEase

Problem: ShopEase required an e-commerce solution capable of handling large volumes of user transactions, dynamic pricing, and real-time inventory management.

Solution: ShopEase leveraged Elixir for its scalability and real-time processing capabilities. The application was built with a microservices architecture, where each service was responsible for a distinct part of the e-commerce functionality.

Key features of the implementation included:

- *User Authentication:* Authentication was handled by a dedicated service using Guardian library for token-based authentication.
- *Product Catalog Management:* Real-time updates to product availability and pricing were orchestrated using GenServer processes to ensure consistent state management.

- *Order Processing:* The order processing pipeline used Broadway for concurrent and resilient processing of orders.
- *Inventory Management:* Real-time inventory updates were managed using distributed Elixir processes, ensuring consistency and availability.

The order processing pipeline is illustrated with the following code snippet:

```
defmodule ShopEase.OrderPipeline do
  use Broadway

  alias Broadway.Message

  def start_link(_opts) do
    Broadway.start_link(__MODULE__,
      name: __MODULE__,
      producer: [
        module: {ShopEase.OrderProducer, []},
        concurrency: 10
      ],
      processors: [
        default: [concurrency: 50]
      ],
      batchers: [
        default: [concurrency: 10, batch_size: 100]
      ]
    )
  end

  def handle_message(_, %Message{} = message, _) do
    # Process order message
    process_order(message.data)
    message
  end

  defp process_order(order_data) do
    # Logic to process order
  end
end
```

Outcome: ShopEase experienced substantial improvements in transaction handling capacity, reducing latency and ensuring smooth operation even during peak shopping periods.

Case Study 3: Financial Services Application

Company: FinanceMax

Problem: FinanceMax needed to build a financial application capable of real-time risk assessment and fraud detection with high computational efficiency and reliability.

Solution: FinanceMax opted for an Elixir-based system due to its robustness and concurrency model. The system architecture was designed to handle real-time data streams and complex analytical computations efficiently.

Significant components included:

- *Real-Time Data Ingestion:* Used Flow for processing streams of transactions in real-time.
- *Risk Calculations:* Employed Task for parallel computation of risk assessment scores.
- *Fraud Detection:* Implemented several pattern matching algorithms using Elixir processes to identify fraudulent transactions.
- *Audit and Logging:* Extensive logging and auditing were handled using Elixir.Logger and external data stores for persistent logs.

Here is an illustrative example of the real-time data ingestion using Flow:

```
defmodule FinanceMax.TransactionFlow do
  alias Experimental.Flow

  def start_link() do
    transactions
    |> Flow.from_enumerable()
    |> Flow.partition()
    |> Flow.reduce(fn -> %{} end, &process_transaction/2)
    |> Flow.run()
  end

  defp process_transaction(transaction, acc) do
    # Perform transaction processing
    Map.put(acc, transaction.id, transaction)
  end
end

transactions = [
  %{id: 1, amount: 100, type: :debit},
  %{id: 2, amount: 200, type: :credit},
  # more transactions
]
```

Outcome: FinanceMax achieved notable accuracy in risk assessment and fraud detection, providing real-time insights that enhanced the service's reliability and customer trust.

These case studies underscore the practical benefits and efficiencies realized with Elixir in diverse application domains, highlighting its scalability, reliability, and performance in production environments.

Made in United States
Orlando, FL
04 November 2026

90202249R00148